My American Dream:

A Journey from

Oppression to Opportunity

By Bernard Reznick

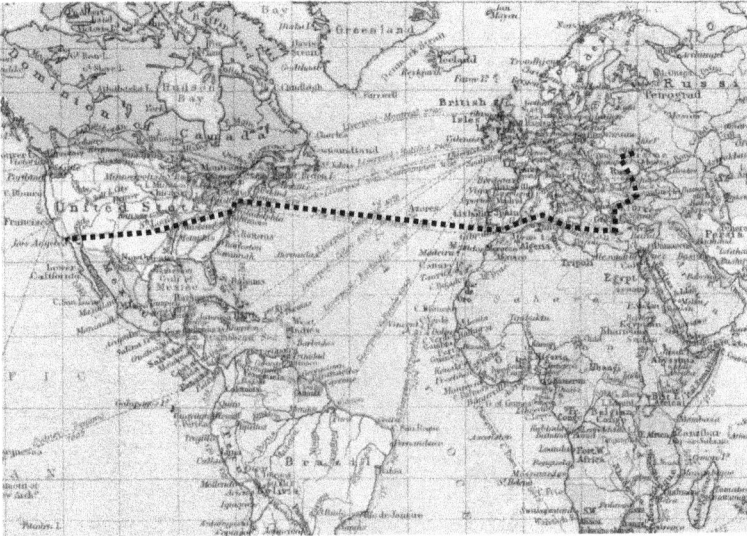

as told to his niece,
Neva Reznick Alderson

edited by his nephew,
Gregory Reznick

About This Book

This book was made possible by Bernie and his niece Neva Reznick Alderson. Neva conducted numerous interviews over a period of several years, taping each one and painstakingly transcribing the conversations into the computer. After she and Bernie had reviewed and revised to the point of exhaustion, Gregory Reznick, Bernie's nephew, edited the document (with an enormous amount of help and support from his wife, Olga) into the form that is presented here.

Contents

Chapter 1: Russia

My story opens at the home of my mother's parents, Eva and Meyer Guravich (Horowitz in English). My grandparents lived in Sobolivka, Russia. In March 1914, I was born Boris Reznick to Mika and Aaron Reznick. My mother had come to her parents' home to bear her first child. My parents' home was Ochrimova, in the province of Kiev, southwest of Uman in the Ukraine. We were Jewish by birth.

My father was a slender man, with dark brown hair who wore a suit with a vest, in which he would carry a gold pocket-watch and chain. He was hardworking and very honest - the most honest man I have ever known. I remember one time he discovered an error on the books of $500 in his favor, and he promptly informed his vendor of the mistake.

My mother was a very pretty lady. She had dirty blonde hair like her sisters, twins Itka and Branchik. Mother had a resolute nature and a keen sense of humor. She liked to tell and play jokes.

My Mother and Father in Russia

Every April Fools' Day, she would tell my brother and me that the school burned down. We would run to the window, from which we could see the school, and she would stand behind us and chuckle. Ma was no dope - nobody put anything over on her. I would say she was the boss of the family. Because I was the eldest, she probably favored me, but after I married, I think she favored my younger brother.

Our village, Ochrimova, was at a crossroads, part of a larger farming estate worked by Russian peasants called "muzhiks". The village and the surrounding lands were owned by a Russian general under Tsar Nicholas II. The Tsar distributed land grants to his generals in return for their support. The more ignorant the people working the lands, the more secure the Tsar felt. The Jewish people, however, had their chaider, which is the educational arm of the synagogue where boys learned the Torah along with reading, writing, arithmetic and other subjects. Thus, upon the ceremony of their bar mitzvah Jewish boys had a basic education. Many continued on to learn more at the chaider. My father studied higher mathematics, which qualified him to be a bookkeeper and accountant for the Russian general in Ochrimova, even though Jews weren't allowed to work for Christians.

Jewish brothers or fathers taught the girls of the family at home. My mother learned the alphabet and learned to read. You could teach yourself, and if you were interested in a particular subject, that's the kind of book you would get. Most of the books my mother read were romance novels. There was an underground system of trading books in the village.

My father managed the general's farming operation. From what my parents told me, the general had a drinking problem and did not pay much attention to business; he relied heavily on my father. We had a good standard of living, especially compared to the muzhiks that had one-room huts with dirt floors and straw roofs. Walls were made of mud mixed with straw and were about a foot thick, and the clay (mud) was used because it was cheaper than lumber. Russia was cold in general, and bitter cold in winter.

We lived in a large clay house painted white, with wood floors and a built-in bench about two feet high around the outside, which also served as a buttress for the walls. My grandmother Reznick, who was a small woman, liked to sit on the bench outside her house wearing her babushka (kerchief) and enjoy the sun. We had a wood-fired oven in the corner of the kitchen, and we used it to bake bread and keep the house warm. My brother and I slept over our oven, which had two pig-iron doors on the front. Through the bottom door they put firewood and the top pig-iron door was to the oven. We climbed to the top of the oven by steps on the side, onto an area about two feet above the oven.

In January 1918, when I was close to four years old, my brother Mulia (later known as Manny or Nick) was born. My father was able to bring a doctor from town to the house, and I was told to be very quiet.

My parents had servants in Ochrimova. We had wood floors, not dirt, and bedrooms. My father was paid well and he bought my

Mother (center rear) and Siblings

mother fine jewelry. I remember an early experience before my brother was born of riding behind a servant on a horse with the wind blowing through my hair. Another experience I remember was straddling a bench with runners on each side. The bench was pulled by a horse, and could accommodate maybe ten people.

In Russia under the Tsar, Jews were not allowed to live in the cities. My father would make periodic shopping trips into Kiev, returning before the curfew of 6:00 PM, when Jews were required to be outside the city walls. One time, my father told me that he had bought a train for me in the city, but on the way home he was robbed and that the robbers now had my train.

I also remember a hold-up at our house. These two fellows wanted to know if we had a gun in the house. My mother said, "No, we don't." I said, "Oh, sure we do," and I showed them where it was, which really saved the day, because they took the gun along with whatever ammunition we had, and left.

The Jews in Russia were technically not allowed to work for anyone else. But because of the synagogue chaider and the education Jewish boys and young men received, they became valuable assets in Russian business operations. My father worked as an accountant and manager for the general, and my mother's father, Meyer Horowitz, managed the sugar mill in his village of Sobolivka.

The Horowitzes

My mother's parents, Grandpa and Grandma Horowitz, had twelve children, eldest to youngest: Leo (Louis), Ruchel (Rachel, Ruth), Morris, Harry, Julius, Anna (Anka), Nathan, Dora, Mika (Mary), the twins Itka and Branchik, and Archic (Archie). There was no security of life for Jews in Russia. There were intermittent pogroms in which Jews were killed as a scapegoat for unrest. About the year 1900 Grandpa Horowitz decided to try his luck in the United States and sailed with his wife and twelve children for the freedom of New York. In the U.S. the Jews had an organization where you went if you had a problem or if you needed to borrow money. The Jews helped other Jews get on their feet. In New York, however, Grandpa Horowitz found the pace too hectic and the language too difficult. He had twelve children and a wife to support. Grandpa

Eva Horowitz, my Grandmother

returned to Sobolivka in 1904 to work at the sugar mill where he got his job back. Back home in Russia, my grandfather had a comfortable position as manager of the sugar mill, where sugar was made from beets that were grown in the area. In his village he may not have felt the oppression against the Jews so strongly, as he lived in a village with other Jewish people as well as non-Jewish people. Probably Grandpa Horowitz was not comfortable working under someone else in the U.S. In Russia, managing the sugar mill in Sobolivka, he was the boss and his family was well-to-do. Five of Grandpa's children stayed in the U.S. Those who stayed in New York were Morris, Harry, Julius, Nathan, and Dora. My mother, who was nineteen, went back to Russia with her father. Dora was sixteen at the time, with a boyfriend, Joe Yaroslav, whom she married. She and her husband Joe had a farm they bought or rented and raised chickens and eggs and stuff. I heard later that after they moved to California, Joe gambled a lot. He was then in the insurance business. Nathan, who was just thirteen, probably stayed with Dora in New Jersey. Morris lived in Boston where he came to be in charge of Metropolitan Life Insurance there. Insurance was an easy job to get because the insurance company didn't have to pay you a salary unless you were in charge of an office. You worked on commission. It's a competitive business and to sell it you have to develop a system of how you get more for your money. Harry lived in Coney Island. Julius went to work in New York, as a cutter of patterns for clothing. Nathan eventually became a wealthy man in the U.S. He and his brother-in-law started the Middlesex Grocery, a wholesale grocery business. New Brunswick is in the county of Middlesex. The business became very well known throughout the state.

The Reznicks

My father's father, my Grandfather Israel Reznick, lived with his wife down the hill, a couple of miles from us, in a house with a clay floor. I remember on Fridays, in preparation for the Sabbath celebration, Grandma would wet the clay floor and it would be like new again.

My father's brother, my Uncle Ben, lived up the street from my grandparents. I don't know what happened to him although I remember he had a son. There was also Aunt Blanche, my father's older sister, who had a son in the revolution, and my father's older brother, Boris, after whom I was named. Boris was tragically killed in a threshing accident before I was born. It was probably a mechanical thresher with cogs and a belt, like a windmill, into which one feeds wheat, drawn by a horse. Boris somehow got caught, or his clothes got caught, in the threshing mechanism. My father was the baby of the family.

Grandmother and Grandfather Reznick

My grandfather Israel Reznick, who had a long red beard, was a broker of livestock, primarily chickens, geese, and sheep. He was a middleman buying from the farmers and selling wholesale to the shopkeepers. My father eventually made his fortune at this business in the United States. The Jews in Russia had to be creative in business. Brokers such as my grandfather were permitted because a muzhik, or recently liberated serf, did not have the education to conduct business, being educationally repressed by the feudal system and thus illiterate. To conduct commerce, the mathematical and entrepreneurial skills of the Jews were needed.

The business of collecting produce from farmers for resale was a time consuming job and required that my grandfather Israel be on the road much of the time going from farm to farm collecting livestock for resale. I saw very little of him.

In the winter my

Yiddish

My parents read Yiddish books written in the Hebrew alphabet, but they didn't speak Hebrew; it was not a home language. Mostly they spoke Russian, and they also spoke Yiddish. Yiddish came in handy. If a Russian Jew met a German Jew they could speak to each other in Yiddish, and I spoke Yiddish when I lived in Russia. You attach words to your language that have become familiar to you and the other people in your neighborhood. For example, say a father gives his son a rent check to deliver to the landlord. The father uses a combination of Yiddish and English to communicate: "*Boychick* (boy), *gay* (go) *downstairs and batzul* (pay) *dem* (the) *real estatenick* (landlord) *de rent.*" But the only Yiddish word is *batzul*.

father and grandfather would slaughter, de-feather, clean and then bury some poultry in the snow to preserve it. We had no mechanical refrigeration. They would make a bed in the snow and layer the meat that they would then cover with snow. On top of that layer they would put some more meat, which they would then cover with snow and so on until there was an ice box of frozen meat which would stay frozen for months. When they wanted a chicken or goose for dinner, they would go to the ice mound and take it out of the "fridge."

The parents of my father and the parents of my mother were on vacation (perhaps in Odessa because Jews were allowed in Odessa), when they met each other and discovered that they had an unmarried son and daughter in turn who could, they considered, marry. Thus my parents' marriage was arranged. It was a practical matter.

Chapter 2: Upheaval

Turn now to the scene of Russia in the early 1900's. World War I broke out in July 1914, four months after I was born. The Russian army was so badly outfitted by the Tsar that though originally involved in the war, the Russian troops quit and went home, signaling the beginning of the Russian Revolution. Conditions in the Russian Army were miserable. Historically, under Nicholas I, there was a compulsory armed service for Jewish boys from twelve to eighteen years old who were delivered to the army by the Kahal (East European communal organization) officials in each Jewish community. There were "khapers" (snatchers) who would prowl through the streets and literally snatch Jewish boys and carry them off to the army, to station them in parts of the country far removed from Jewish influence. They were recruiters. Over there, they didn't ask you if you wanted to join. In order to avoid the army men in my father's time (including my father) would sometimes shoot themselves in the hand so they wouldn't be able to pull a trigger, or have their teeth pulled out so they couldn't eat the sawdust that substituted for food in the Russian Army.

World War I ended in November of 1918, but the Russians had gone home long before that, and the Russian Revolution started in the same month. The revolution

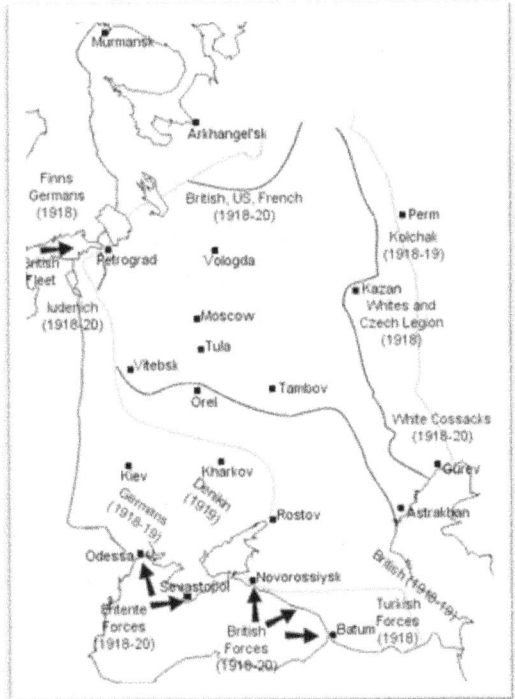

had been simmering since 1905, after the war between Russia and Japan. President Theodore Roosevelt helped settle the dispute, but it came out that the Tsar was giving away land to the generals and stuff like that. As long as they were ignorant there was nothing they could do. Once the population began to think a little, the revolutionaries started having meetings and inviting people to listen at the meetings. Finally the Tsar was killed, and there was no head of state. The Tsar had been a fool. His generals were fools as well — their greed exceeded their experience. They sent an army into World War I without guns, without uniforms, and without any reason to fight. A lot of the soldiers left the war front and came home. They weren't being fed. They were just out there fighting a war that they didn't know what the heck it was about, and after the soldiers returned home they were active in the revolutionary meetings. The soldiers asked, "Why are you sending me to be killed? You don't give me anything to protect myself!" And here's a guy who says, "I can tell you why: you are being kept in ignorance so you don't know anything. Here is communism that can offer you a better life than Tsarism...now, do you want a better life or don't you?" As bad as communism is compared to democracy, it's better than Tsarism.

In 1919, when my brother Manny was one and a half and I was five and a half, we packed up and went first to our grandparents' Horowitz in Sobolivka. From there my father went on to Uman to set things up for us. He did what had to be done. To survive, he had to think ahead. So in 1920, we went to the good-sized city of Uman, which with the fall of Tsar Nicholas was now open to Jews. Great domestic turmoil was underway as the organized government in Russia broke down. The Russian general who owned Ochrimova and the surrounding area - and for whom my father had worked as a bookkeeper - committed suicide because life as he had known it came to an end. The peasants were in rebellion, and he, as a large landholder, was doomed. The general had created a frustration among the muzhiks, because the Jews were involved in running the show. So when the revolution broke out and the general committed suicide, (remember this isn't just little happenings...this is turmoil), the muzhiks took out their frustration against the Jews.

My parents knew it was time to make a move. On his shopping trips to Kiev, my father began converting his rubles to gold and diamonds, a more secure form of exchange. We packed up our horse and wagon and left Ochrimova and my father's parents forever. They were later killed in a revolutionary pogrom, where unarmed Jewish civilians were killed by soldiers to let off steam.

During the Tsar's time, pogroms were encouraged because they kept the ignorant populace quiet. They were made to feel superior to the Jews. The Jews were merely being used as an escape. The Tsar needed a distraction, a scapegoat, because if the muzhiks realized that he was giving their land away to the generals, making them rich so they would protect him at the expense of the muzhiks, it would be bad for the Tsar. So he said, "Wait a minute, it's not the general's fault, it's the Jews' fault." Who were they going to kill? My father was no longer there, but his parents were. Whatever Jews were in the village of Ochrimova were probably killed. The Jews that survived in that time joined up with the Bolsheviks. The Communist Manifesto is very liberal toward Jews. However, Russian communism did not favor Jews. In fact, they maintained the same attitude as the Tsar. The Marxist philosophy toward Jews was there, but not the practice.

They say, "you can't teach an old dog new tricks." The great majority of the populace of Russia was Russians who were previously taught to kill Jews. Now, all of a sudden, they're supposed to love 'em? Anti-Semitism is under the skin almost everywhere.

Over the years, my mother would hear from her sister Branchik, Itka's twin, about what was going on. After World War II started, her father died and her mother traveled to Kharkov with her daughter Branchik and Branchik's daughters Mara and Tamara as well as Eva's son Archik, fleeing from the Germans; they went east. Someone must have gone first, telling them, "I'm in Kharkov, come to Kharkov." You just don't go someplace blindly. You always need connections.

In Uman my father bought a seltzer water factory and we stayed in Uman for about two and a half years. When one of the factory workers broke a leg due to an explosion of a carbon dioxide container, my father sold the factory and my parents began another business. They opened a delicatessen in the front part of our house, selling mostly salami.

My mother began to understand that food is good business. One, you have to eat. Two, other people have to eat. Salami was a good product because it did not spoil. To my mother, salami was legal tender. One could buy a lot of it at one time and keep it in the closet. It had a skin on it, so if it got a little moldy it didn't matter because you could just wipe off the mold and it was still good. It might, over time, shrink because of a loss of fat, lowering its poundage. One would have to take that into consideration when it was priced for sale. For example, a ten pound salami, might, with less fat, shrink to a nine pound salami with the same amount of meat. When things were quiet, people would come to buy a salami.

My mother became adept at handling challenging situations. In Uman at that time, different factions were struggling for power. There were the Bolsheviks (which meant the majority) and the Mensheviks (which mean the minority). There were many religious groups in the struggle, some of whom were anti-Semitic. You never knew who would come through and be knocking at your door or what they would want. When the knock came from belligerent soldiers, my mother would say, "Hey guys, take it easy. Sit down. Have a salami sandwich and some tea. Eat. Relax. Take some sandwiches for the road." The soldiers ate, relaxed, and hit the road with their "to go" items.

While my parents were busy running the delicatessen, it was my job to take care of my little brother. One time when Mulia was two and a half, and I was off-duty, he decided to go downtown. Not being able to say Mulia Reznick when asked his name, he said what sounded like "Moochnick." The people who helped him took him to the Moochnicks who said, "Oh yes we know him, he's a Reznick." and took him home.

The housing in Uman was around a courtyard. There was a square block of houses, each facing the street with their backs to the courtyard. There were two large fortress-like gates opening into the courtyard which were always closed and locked. The people of the courtyard formed a community. The young men of different courtyards were rival gangs. One time I remember bricks being hurled over our courtyard door gates by enemies. To me it was a game, and I was interested in seeing what was going to happen. I wasn't frightened by it. My mother wouldn't let me outside while they were fighting each other. Personally, I've never felt like joining a gang, but apparently a lot of people do. In this case, the people identified with the courtyard and banded together for protection, to the point where other bands were enemies and there would be skirmishes.

Since the Russian Army had capitulated in World War I, when we arrived the area was under German occupation. The war was over, but the Germans were still there. They were asked to stay there and take care of things until the arrangements were made for their removal. German soldiers patrolled the streets of Uman, keeping order. I remember they were there and then all of a sudden they weren't there. After the Germans left, there was turmoil. Once there was a man killed in the street outside our courtyard and people were afraid to pull him out of the street because they didn't want to get shot themselves. They didn't know who killed him or why. I didn't know the guy. They got his body at night. You might get killed even if you were a good guy to the shooters because they might not know that and think it was safer to shoot you. So there were pogroms going on and there were revolutions going on. I remember people going around shooting people. Nothing that was happening, however, made me afraid of anything. As far as I was concerned, that's how the world was.

Often the Jews were made scapegoats for the errors and frustrations of the Russian generals. The Jews were charged with pro-German sympathies. As the Russian Civil War dragged on, it grew increasingly bitter and bloody, and with it the "Whites" (anti-communists) directed a mounting savagery against the Jews. It was a seesaw: the "Reds" (communists) would take a town one day; the Whites would retake it the next. The first act of the Whites would be to initiate a pogrom, accusing the Jews of sympathy for the Reds.

My parents decided to apply for entry into the United States of America. We would have a sponsor, since my mother had five siblings in America from her father's previous emigration. But because a quota system was now in place we would have to wait our turn. It was relatively quiet in Uman - a good time to get a move on toward a better place. The situation in Russia looked bleak: society was in upheaval and a revolution was going on. The government had been overthrown, the Tsar and his family executed. The future was uncertain and the struggle for power immense.

Chapter 3: Exodus

We were planning to leave Russia. We planned to sneak across the border into Bessarabia, now called Moldova, an area near the Ukraine, between Russia and Romania, and which is a long, narrow, formerly Russian disputed territory. At this time the Romanians were claiming it as their territory. We had to wait for winter to depart Uman because we didn't have a boat, and we had to cross the river Dniester into Bessarabia after the river froze, into the border town of Krimenetz. There were people who would sneak you across for a fee, taking a lot of people across at one time. It was a two or three-day journey from Uman to the river.

The capitol of Bessarabia was Kishenev (now Chişinău). Because Bessarabia kept changing ownership at that time between the Russians and the Romanians, you didn't have to have identification papers because you could claim to be a citizen of either side and no one could challenge you. If you didn't have Romanian identification papers, officials would give them to you, as the territory was newly claimed as Romanian.

We had furniture in the house in Uman, so my parents hired a drayman with a wagon and we put our bedding and whatever other furniture we could in the wagon. I don't know why they thought they could ever get it across the border. I remember there were two horses pulling this wagon loaded with furniture. We were sitting on the bedding. The wagon took us to Sobolivka, which was on the way from Uman to the border, where we said goodbye to my grandparents. The arrangement was that they were going to deliver our merchandise to us somewhere in Bessarabia once we told them where to deliver it, but of course they never did. They may have left some of the stuff with my grandparents.

I was almost six years old and Mulia was not yet three. I remember my grandmother ran things - she was a Jewish mother, and in her house, she was the lady of the house. This was the last time I saw my grandparents, and the last time my mother saw her parents.

We rode the wagon to the assembly point. From there I had to walk to the border and my mother had to carry Mulia. I remember holding my mother's hand and walking across a frozen wasteland until we got to the river. I wasn't afraid. My mother gave me a sense of security.

Our father had gone ahead to establish a base for us in Krimenetz. He probably rented some rooms. So it was just the three of us struggling to get to the frozen river, traveling by night and hiding in haystacks by day, for two nights and one day. The border patrol knew what was going on and would periodically check the haystacks where we were hiding by poking them with pitch forks. As the story went, every now and then, a mother would smother her child to keep it from crying and revealing the hiding place. "You know so and so, she strangled her own baby." It was a very difficult time. If we were discovered, it was the end of the road.

We came to the border at dawn after the second night of walking. We were then guided across the frozen river into Bessarabia. We arrived at a little town called Kriminetz on the border of Bessarabia. Kriminetz reminds me now of a gold rush town, with people running about unsettled and going somewhere. It was winter. Once in Bessarabia we were okay, because you could speak either Romanian or Russian and get away with it. But we couldn't find my father, and discovered that he was in jail. My mother went and bailed him out, possibly with a diamond and a gold ring or something. The police were corrupt and would snatch people off the streets and release them for money. Maybe he didn't have any money. Maybe my mother had it all. My mother knew how to work the system.

From Kriminetz we went to Kishenev, the capitol of Moldova and a well-established, small city, where we found a small apartment, which was some rooms in a house. The buildings in Kishenev were well-constructed and more modern than in the villages. My parents kept going by selling my mother's jewelry. After we rented the rooms, Dad looked for a place to rent as a store, and he came across a strategically located cave.

My parents started a produce/deli in this small cave that he rented and they did very well. The cave-deli, which was in a hill, was a popular place on the main street, which ended at a big hospital that took up a lot of room. The hospital was on a large lot at the end of a streetcar line. The cave, between our apartment house and another house, was in a strategic spot because it accommodated people who worked at the big hospital as well as visitors coming to the hospital.

My dad cleaned the cave out, built a counter, and put in electricity. He started to sell produce such as watermelon and grapes. Then he started putting in groceries, like sugar and flour. Soon my folks were selling salami sandwiches.

After my parents ran the cave business for a while, we moved down the street to another apartment house with a courtyard that was owned by the same people that rented us the cave. They lived in a big house at the end of the street and had a son who became my friend.

The streetcar conductor would let my friend and me drive the streetcar at the end of the line,

Family Portrait

where the tracks of different directions merged into one track. While he went to get a cup of coffee, we switched the overhead wire from one line to the other line, going in the opposite direction. Then we would take the driving handles off, and move them to the opposite end of the car.

At the other end of the streetcar line was a train station, as in most European cities. There were no cars. There were taxis, but they were drawn by horses, like they have in New York's Central Park. Cars had been developed but they were not prevalent. If there were no gas stations around, what good is a car? You also had to have roads, and it took time before that developed.

The building where we stayed was built around a courtyard shared by a block of houses, as is common in Europe. The courtyard had a big fortress-like gate like the gates of our courtyard in Uman. In Kishenev we didn't have an oven but we had a stove. It had a place for the wood to go in and you left the door open. It wasn't that big a house, but the heat wasn't radiated out all over like an oven.

While my parents were working at their store, I was in charge of watching Mulia. It was not that easy, as he was energetic, wiry, and elusive, always on the move. One time when he was four and I was about eight, I went in the house for a minute and he disappeared. Suddenly, some kid falls out of the apple tree in the courtyard! I never thought to look for him in the apple tree. I didn't know he could even climb the tree. Manny was bleeding badly from a wound in his head! I was bewildered and didn't know what to do. The folks around took care of him and someone went to tell my mother what had happened. She came and took care of him, but did I get a spanking! That's the way they took care of frustration in those days. And this is what became known as "the apple tree incident."

I went to school in Kishenev and studied the Romanian alphabet which was different from the Russian alphabet, which is the Cyrillic alphabet. The Romanian alphabet was the same as English, making it much easier when I got to the U.S. to learn English. Kishenev felt safe. I remember seeing my first movie there. A good movie to me had to have a train going through it. Trains represented adventure.

We didn't have contact with relatives in general except through correspondence. But the Loshaks - a family of second cousins on my father's side - were in Kishenev with us, also waiting for their quota notice. They may have been the people who told us to go to Kishenev to wait for our papers to emigrate. The Loshaks' sponsor was in Mexico, so they ended up living in Monterrey, Mexico. Around 1938, the Loshaks immigrated again to the United States, and came to Los Angeles. I don't know if they had a sponsor. At that time, people could get into the States if they had money, and would therefore not become a burden to the government. The Loshaks had three children, and I think their daughter Esther was born in Mexico, because I don't remember her in Kishenev. Esther was a pretty young woman and she had a very interested suitor in Monterrey, Isador, who followed her to Los Angeles in pursuit. He had a business to maintain in Mexico, so he would come up on weekends. He succeeded, and at the wedding in Los Angeles, in 1939, our four-year old son, Marvin, was the ring bearer. Isador and Esther would come up from Mexico to Los Angeles to visit Esther's parents and they would call us when they were in town. By interesting coincidence, Isador turned out to be a relative of my wife, Sadie. Isador and Esther had three children, but they suffered a tragedy when one of their kids was swept out to sea by a tsunami in Acapulco and was never seen again.

Chapter 4: Passage

We were in Kishenev for about two years, from 1920 to 1923. When we got our quota notice we left in winter, around February 1, 1923. We went by train from Kishenev to Bucharest, the capitol of Romania, where we spent two days. That's where the American consulate was, and where we picked up our papers from the American Ambassador to Romania. When our number came up to be granted entry into the United States after waiting two and a half years, Nathan Horowitz, our mother's brother who had

The Braga

remained in the U.S. after his father Meyer's return to Russia, sent our visas and prepaid tickets for our passage on a ship called the "Braga" to the American Consulate in Bucharest.

From Bucharest we went to Constanza, the only Romanian port on the Black Sea, and boarded the Braga, a converted freighter not designed for passengers. The freight area was converted to steerage. It took us 30 days to travel by ship from Constanza to New York, and we went in steerage. Steerage (down below deck), where the freight normally went, consisted of bunkers with four bunk beds in each bunker. There were two bunk beds on each side, strung all over, and we had one bunker. People bought, brought, or rented some kind of blankets to hang up for privacy because it was open. The area was about 8 x 8 feet, so it was pretty tight. Underneath the bed there was room to shove any belongings you had, maybe two suitcases of clothes.

Our first stop was Istanbul, which was called Constantinople at the time. Everyone aboard ship was taken to a steam bath so that when we boarded again we were all clean. From there we went down the Black Sea through the Bosporus Strait, into the Sea of Marmara, through the Dardanelles Strait, into the Aegean Sea, down into the Mediterranean Sea, through the Mediterranean down to the Straits of Gibraltar, and through the Straits up to Lisbon. From Lisbon we crossed the Atlantic Ocean to land at Ellis Island in New York.

The Bosporus Strait divides Europe from Asia, East from West. The Reznicks thus crossed from the world of the East to the world of the West. In Russia the dominant religion was Eastern Orthodox. They did not use the Gregorian calendar which we follow here. For example, the Eastern Orthodox religion has Christmas twelve days later. My birthday had actually been some time in February, but in order to transfer the date of my birthday it was changed to March 3rd. And Mulia must have been born twelve days earlier than the birthday that we always celebrated on January 4, 1918.

From Lisbon it was difficult crossing the north Atlantic in February. Fortunately, I was not affected by seasickness, and one time I showed up for breakfast and I was the only one who showed up! I had my ninth birthday on board the ship and my father bought me a caramel candy for a nickel...which I enjoyed very much.

Our Immigration photo

We arrived in New York on March 5, 1923 and awoke to see the statue of Liberty. We were delivered to Ellis Island on March 6th, where we were placed in quarantine for two days in a cubicle like a jail cell. Uncle Nathan came from New Brunswick, New Jersey to pick us up. He cleared us for entry and we went home with him on March 7th.

Nathan and Celia

Nathan was able to sign for us as our immigration sponsor. As a sponsor, he signed that we would not be charges to the government for any reason. In other words, we wouldn't ask for government aid. He guaranteed that if we required help, he would have to provide it. In our family immigration photo we are wearing identical shirts my mother had made for us. (They were really blouses from a pattern she had.) My family took the ferry with Uncle Nathan to New York from Ellis Island and we traveled to New Brunswick in his Model-T Ford — it was pretty fancy.

We came to this country and my mother had four brothers and one sister here and they were family. I never knew them before but they were special people. You didn't look at it as they were good people or bad people, ugly people or beautiful people, whatever; they were family. That was the attitude of my parents toward them and so you pick up the same feeling from them. If you made a list of all the people you liked, family would be at the top. (When Manny and I were on the outs, it bothered me that something happened to make me have that experience. But if he hadn't been my brother, it wouldn't have bothered me half as much.)

Uncle Nathan was one of our mother's younger brothers. He and his brother-in-law, Aunt Celia's brother, owned a big, well-known wholesale grocery business which is still in existence today, called The Middlesex Wholesale Grocery. I remember he also had a lot of sacks of sugar, beans, salt and stuff like that. Uncle Nathan had a son, Barney, who was my brother Mulia's age. Barney acted "uppity," as we were the "greenhorns." My mother's sister, Aunt Itka, also came to the United States

Outhouses and Washing Machines

When we came to the United States in 1923, there were still outhouses. The backyard was where the outhouse was. That was it.

In the twenties, when we came, the middle class was beginning to get toilets. Uncle Nathan had a toilet. We didn't. However, after a couple of years they started putting them in. The lower class, they had to wait awhile.

When we first came to New Brunswick you would generally wind up in what they call a "court." They would have a half a dozen or dozen apartments with one or two outhouses.

The Mexican courtyards with patios still had outhouses. Washing and taking baths was done at the sink. In the early days we would boil water. We had laundry tubs and we used to do the laundry in them. Put your laundry in there, with soap and hot water. If you want to have a bath, you get some hot water and you mix it with cold water because you couldn't stand the hot water by itself.

You would sit in this tub and you would wash yourself. You wash your hair in the sink. After the first two years here, my dad already had some money. We had our own bathroom. I remember our first washing machine came with a wringer. When you got through washing, you would wring it out. Then you take the damp clothes and hang them up in the backyard.

about a month earlier than us. She had been around town in Kishenev. She got married at around seventeen and she and her husband Max came to visit us in Uman.

Dora, my mother's other sister who had stayed after her father's original emigration, lived in Atlantic City with her husband and three children. We visited her and she Americanized my name to Bernard. My mother, Mika, had become Mary and my brother, Mulia, had become Emmanuel during our immigration. Mulia is a common Russian name. Louis, the oldest brother of my mother, had a son named Mulia also. They were probably named after a relative. (We named our daughter Barbara after Sadie's father, Bertalon. My son Marvin was named after my grandfather Mayer Horowitz.)

Uncle Nathan had a very nice house with an indoor toilet, which was very impressive at that time. We quickly got our own apartment and lived as frugally as we could. We didn't know the language; however my mother could read English and remembered some words from when she had lived in the states for four years with her father and mother during her youth. She was fourteen when she came to the U.S. in 1900 and eighteen when she went back to Russia. She went back in 1904 and was married in 1912 at 26. She was a self-educated woman. She was able to learn English rapidly in New Brunswick this time and there were also plenty of immigrants to translate for us.

Mother and Dora

My father got a job with the Michelin Tire Company outside of New Brunswick and he worked there manufacturing tires for about a year, saving every nickel he could. We lived in a Jewish community, about three blocks away from Uncle Nathan and Aunt Celia. When you are an immigrant in new surroundings it is nice to be among people with whom you have something in common, who speak the same language. My mother began sewing for people and put out a sign that said "French Seamstress."

Chapter 5: East Coast Adventures

There was interaction in New Brunswick between the Italian, Polish, Hungarian and Jewish communities who shared a common downtown. It was a very nice little downtown. It had three movies and a dry goods store; it had all kinds of different kinds of stores. It's not that big a town. On the other side was Rutgers University and all of the mansions of the town. We had a river. We had a bridge. The last house we lived in was an apartment. There was a group of apartments. I think there were three or four buildings and each building had I believe four apartments. It had a yard, but not like the European courtyard.

Eventually my father struck out on his own, starting his own business. He bought a horse and wagon and rented a barn to house them, not far from where we lived. He started buying crates of oranges and peddled them door-to-door. Little by little he developed two or three routes which he covered on different days of the week and he expanded into a variety of fruits and vegetables. He developed a very nice business as a peddler, selling produce, going out to country places where it was convenient for people to buy good quality fruit off the wagon. He had a good following. In the summer, when school was out, I would go with him every day. Many Jewish immigrants took up peddling.

My father found a market and created customers by providing regular service and offering a consistently good product. He expanded his product based on demand. He catered to people. His horse knew the routes so well that while my father was completing business with one customer, the horse would take the wagon to the next house, where the customer would come out to check out the fresh fruit and determine their purchase. My father liked working for himself and had started his own business as soon as he could. At the beginning, while he was saving, we lived in pretty crummy places. My parents were thrifty. We were in New Brunswick for six years. We moved about five times, to better and better places. I was there from '23 to '29, from age nine to fourteen. At that age, six years is a life time. I made some friends who came out to L.A. and looked me up as an adult. The produce business went very well. My father sold the horse and wagon and bought a truck in 1928.

Because I went to school, I learned English quickly. I started out in kindergarten at nine years old. The principal in New Brunswick at Lord Sterling Elementary didn't know what to do with me so she, Mrs. Whitlock, put me in kindergarten and told the teacher to evaluate me. About two weeks later I was in first grade. Then I went to summer school and when I came back I was in the second grade, still nine years old.

I was doing pretty well. We were in a Jewish neighborhood and the teacher assigned Sol Seid, who later became a congressman from New Jersey, to be my mentor. He spoke Yiddish and if I had a question, I was to ask him. What does this mean, what does that mean? By the time summer came around, I spoke very well. I went on my own to summer school and did third grade. When I went back to school in the fall, I was in the fourth grade, which was the right level for a ten year old. The fourth grade teacher was good and happened to be the aunt of Joyce Kilmer, a well known poet who wrote the famous poem, Trees.

Because I had learned English, my father of necessity depended on me to help him understand the American world around him. For example, my dad subscribed to the Jewish paper called Forward. The paper referred to American situations by the American name, like "prohibition." It assumed that you knew what "prohibition" meant. Or sometimes they referred to it as the "nineteenth amendment." What the heck does that mean? I understood American terminology and I could clarify it for him.

When I was in New Brunswick when I was about 13, shortly after my bar mitzvah, I answered an ad for help in a silk thread processing factory. It was across town, about two miles from our house (I had to walk wherever I wanted to go). This was a summer job and I would work in the afternoons. Since I was now a "working man," my mother gave me a quarter for lunch. I went to a deli where I got two corned beef sandwiches and a coke for 25 cents. I had lunch before reporting for work.

I enjoyed working. I found work interesting. Apparently the factory bought silk which was delivered to them in bundles. What I did was put these bundles into a washing machine and added a prearranged amount of oil. Then I would turn a machine on and it would wash the silk thread with oil. In the process of washing it reached a spin cycle and spun off the oil into a container. When the machine stopped automatically, I took the oil washed silk and put it into a hamper. There were about 20 women sitting at machines that would come up and get a bundle of silk and work a machine that wound it on large spools which were then apparently sold to factories making silk hosiery or other silk items. By working I was contributing to the family. I never kept the money; I gave the money to my mother.

Working was something that was expected for some sort of success. Another of the first paying jobs I got was in 1928, at fourteen years old, while I was in Roosevelt Jr. High in New Brunswick. This was five years after we arrived and one year before we moved to Philadelphia. My dad got me a job at Davidson's supermarket on Fridays and Saturdays in downtown New Brunswick. This was a very fancy store. Their biggest customers were the professors and so on at Rutgers University who had their groceries delivered to their home. I lived at the other end of town and walked to work. It was a small town so it wasn't a long walk, about ten minutes.

My dad was in the produce business. He bought produce from the wholesale market downtown. This fellow was the buyer for produce for Davidson's and he knew my father, becoming acquainted with him at 4:00 in the mornings at the produce market. Maybe he said something to my dad that they needed a kid. So my dad might have said, "How 'bout my son?" The only thing I know is that my father told me to go and see him. So I went over there after school and I asked for him. He was expecting me.

He looked me over and said, "What experience do you have?' I said, "Me, I don't have any experience. I worked with my father on the wagon." He says, "I can't hire you without some experience." I said, "Well, how do you expect anyone to get experience unless they get hired first?" He laughed and said, "Okay, I'll give you a chance." So he told me to come on Friday after school which I did.

He took me around and showed me what to do. Whatever they told me to do, I did conscientiously. He took me downstairs and showed me how to clean produce. That was his department and he's the guy that hired me so that's where I belonged. So I was down there maybe two or three weeks, working with the produce that had come, washing and trimming the celery and the lettuce and washing and making bundles out of the radishes.

I was down there maybe two or three weeks when I volunteered to help one of the guys. I helped him load the truck; he was ready to pick up orders one day but the orders weren't made up. Maybe the person who filled the orders had quit. The orders came on the phone; whoever took the orders wrote them down. Then someone made them up. The basement had pretty much the same inventory as they had upstairs. I didn't have to go upstairs to fill the orders. So here he was ready to pick up orders and they weren't made so somebody gave me one to fill. Well, I got to the point where I knew where everything was so I was able to fill the orders a lot faster than the people upstairs because they never did this. Mr. Davidson, the owner, looked at me and knew he could depend on me. He promoted me to the order clerk so I was no longer cleaning produce. I was filling orders.

At first he went downstairs a couple of times to see if the orders were correct and they were. We didn't have everything downstairs. Once in a while I had to go upstairs to get an item to fill an order. Over a period of time I got an idea of where everything was. So I'm upstairs picking up an item and Mr. Davidson came over and said, "What are you doing up here?" I said, "Well, we don't have this downstairs." He said, "Do you get calls for this very often?" I said "No." He said, "How did you know it was here?" I said, "Well, I had to find out." Anyway, he was very impressed with me and after that he always gave me a pat on the back, which for him was a show of affection. I worked there until we left for Philadelphia.

Meanwhile, my father had a friend, Louis Rom, from Ochrimova in Philadelphia, Pennsylvania, who owned a factory that manufactured ladies' bloomers. My dad had a few bucks and his friend talked him into going in with him. I didn't help in the factory. What could I do? I didn't know how to sew. Machines made things. Before moving there I finished out my school year in New Brunswick, staying with my Aunt Itka from April until June. I had a girl friend in New Brunswick but it didn't mean anything. I looked on the move to Philadelphia as an adventure. I had a pretty good time in Philadelphia.

It probably would have worked out except that it was 1929, the year of the great stock market crash that started the Great Depression. That killed everything. My dad lost most of his money and he and his friend lost the bloomer business in less than one year. I spent one semester of high school, ninth grade, in Philadelphia.

About midterm my dad bought a grocery store from whatever he could salvage out of that mess. My father went to Atlantic City, New Jersey, about sixty miles away, to buy a grocery store because it was available. Some broker told him about it. It was the right price and in the right neighborhood. It was strategically located in a middle class residential area, and was set up and stocked as a typical "Mom and Pop" store. We dealt in groceries, cigarettes, ice cream and whatever else a little grocery store might have. We bought the store and leased the property. Remember, with a deli or grocery store, you always had something to eat, which is important in any kind of a stress situation. They bought it because I was supposed to have experience from the supermarket where I worked in New Brunswick. They depended on my judgment. They shouldn't have, but they did for the names of things they weren't familiar with. Under normal conditions you don't depend on a fifteen-year-old's judgment! But I did know the brands. Don't forget they were grown-up adults that came from Europe; they didn't know the brand names or anything else about it. Well, I had become familiar with different things that people bought. They depended on my knowledge of brand names like "Kellogg" or this name or brand name for the coffee; whatever. What to buy for the store, what deli items to have, what meat to have, how to slice it. It was quite different than just selling salami.

Again, I saw the move to Atlantic City as another adventure. We got there in the summer and I was the salesman in the store. My father, trying to improve the store, would go to the big chicken and egg-producing area between Philadelphia and Atlantic City, getting fresh eggs at wholesale prices for our store and an occasional chicken now and then that was "on order."

The store in Atlantic City was at the basement level, which was the street level. It was a four-story building. We had the top floor for ourselves with two bedrooms and a bathroom. There were a lot of stairs to go up to the fourth floor. We just slept up there.. The third floor was broken down into rooms by the landlady and in the summer she rented them out for a week or two or a month at a time. The building was more or less empty during the winter but she made up for it in the summer. The landlady lived on the floor above the store, the second floor. Downstairs on the first floor, behind the store, was a big dining room/kitchen/living room and a bathroom. We had a bell on the door to the store, so if my mother was busy in the kitchen and heard the bell, she would come out and wait on the customer. The store/apartment where we lived in Atlantic City was in a nice residential neighborhood just a block or two away from the ocean. The city is very long and narrow, about a mile wide and 12 miles long, so no matter where you lived, you were pretty close to the ocean.

We were in Atlantic City for almost two years. I spent my sophomore and part of my junior year in high school there. For a while

I was an usher in a movie house. The friends I had made in Philadelphia came with their families to Atlantic City in the summer months and they looked me up and we had fun. We did a lot of swimming. Sometimes we had our own areas so we could find each other.

Aunt Dora, who had meanwhile moved to Los Angeles, kept saying, "Come on out here!" The Depression was still on and a little grocery store wouldn't do too well unless it did some things that the big chain, A & P, would not. My father sold on credit, which the A & P did not, thus he could compete.

Sex Education

On Friday nights we would meet at one of the girls' houses: different Fridays, different houses. We would listen to the radio and then we would neck. In the necking process the only thing they allowed was to touch the breasts. It was a breakthrough in a manner of speaking. The girls were relatively smart. In allowing that to happen, and preventing anything else from happening, it gave you the opportunity to enter into the sexual world to some extent.

Even though we got aroused and wanted to do more, they wouldn't allow it. So it made them nice girls to the extent that they knew that this had to happen. There was a barrier. Once a girl went to bed with somebody, her reputation was damaged; it was over with. Necking with somebody was one thing. Going to bed with somebody was a totally different thing.

Neither they nor we were ready for anything beyond breast touching. It was a nice thing for all of us.

We met at their houses when their parents were gone. They said they were going to have a party without going into detail. The girls controlled the situation. We would sit in different chairs with the girls on our laps. It was a pre-determined way to break through the sexual barrier without creating any kind of problem. It didn't become a one girl, one guy situation. We switched around on different nights. None of the girls ever became "girl friends" that I know of.

When we first got to the houses we'd talk awhile, and listen to music a while, and then one of the girls would come over and sit in your lap or something, or maybe you invited somebody. As far as I was concerned this was a normal procedure in the development of your sexuality.

Chapter 6: Westward Ho!

Ma and Pa decided to go out to Los Angeles after a year and a half. The business in Atlantic City went all right for a while but in 1930 the Depression was getting worse and worse all the time and having given a lot of people credit who weren't able to make payment, my father couldn't pay his own bills and decided we had to get out. We couldn't even sell the store; we auctioned everything off. We accumulated a little money. In Los Angeles your living expenses were considerably less. Because it was warm you didn't have to buy coal to keep warm or two sets of clothes and two sets of shoes or whatever. It was cheaper. We had family there but we would have to make it on our own.

Aunt Dora beckoned, "The living is easier here in California." Aunt Itka was there waiting for us

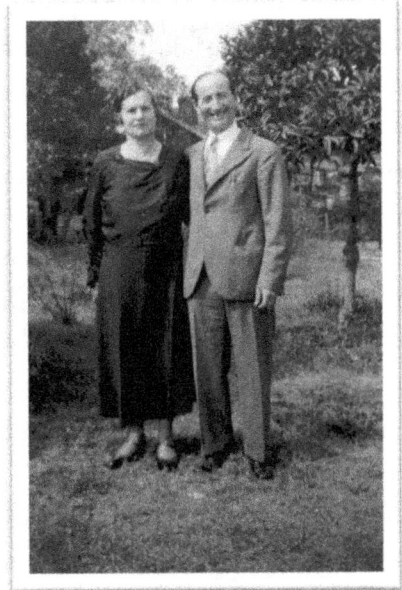

Ma and Pa

when we arrived. She had stayed in New Brunswick when we were in Philadelphia and in Atlantic City but when we went to L.A., she also went. I suspect the family of Max, her husband, who were well off in Connecticut, helped financially to make the move.

We started the drive to California from New Jersey in December of 1930 when I was about 14. The car was a new, blue, 1929 Plymouth, which Dad had acquired in Philadelphia when he was a salesman for the bloomers company. When the company was liquidated, Dad wound up with the car and that was what we drove to Atlantic City and then drove out to California. We had loaded the car with everything from the store that we didn't sell, so we had a whole case of coffee in the trunk.

The trip from Atlantic City to Los Angeles took about ten days. We were traveling in the winter, so there were some areas that were pretty cold, but we took what was called the "Southern Route". We went through Texas and Arizona, hoping to hit warmer weather. One night we stayed in an inn in Lafayette, Arkansas. We had our breakfast, went outside to the car, and the engine was frozen! There was a piece of ice sticking up out of the radiator with the cap on top! Not only had the frozen water expanded, it had managed to unscrew the cap to have somewhere to go! We set a barbeque up in front of the car and thawed it out. The water melted and we were ready to roll. And this was supposed to be the warm south!

My dad was driving day and night so to speak, but I was allowed to drive a bit in Mississippi. There was nobody else on the road, so I guess my dad figured it would be all right. I was driving along pretty well but suddenly I swerved for some reason - I think I hit a pothole in the road - and we wound up in a ditch. I don't know where all these people came from, but there must have been 30 or 40 black people that came running from all parts of the road to see what they could do to help us. They looked things over and saw that there was no damage but noted that we couldn't drive out of there. They literally lifted the car out of the ditch and put it back on the road. I started the engine. It worked! To thank them we gave them each a can of coffee. My dad got back behind the wheel and off we went. It was a long drive; at the time there were no freeways.

When we arrived in Los Angeles after a couple of weeks on the road, staying in motels along the way, we resided for a week with the widow of Uncle Nathan, Aunt Celia. Nathan had died of tuberculosis at the age of 33 (a couple of years after our arrival in the US). My aunt sold out and moved west. She bought a 12-unit flat in Los Angeles on North Hicks Street with the money from the grocery business in New Brunswick. My aunt remarried when she came to California. She married a man with the last name of Stein, and Aunt Celia always referred to him as "Stein." I don't remember his first name for that reason. He was a very nice man.

He was in wholesale produce and gave me a job in the summertime. One time we were unloading watermelons. I remember there was a guy on top of my uncle's truck. He would throw the watermelons to one guy who would throw them to me, and I would put the watermelon on the ground, or stack it. We were unloading watermelons that we were delivering to a store. I got distracted and I dropped a watermelon. I thought, "Oh my gosh, I'll get fired, my parents will beat me up!" Stein came over and said, "Don't worry about it. We'll take it home and eat it...don't worry about it. These things happen." He was very nice about it. In those days a watermelon might have cost ten cents, which was a lot of money. It was terrible.

We stayed in Aunt Celia's 12-flat in City Terrace on Hicks for a week and I went to school with Sam, the boy who lived across the hall in the building, renting from Aunt Celia. It was through Sam that I met my future wife Sadie who lived on Pomeroy in City Terrace, a few blocks away. I met her almost as soon as I got to L.A. We rented a little house in January of '31, on Blanchard Street, about two blocks away.

The place on Blanchard Street consisted of a front room (living room/dining room combination) where I slept on a cot. Manny slept on a cot in the kitchen and my parents slept in the bedroom. There was a bathroom off the kitchen.

After a year on Blanchard, early in '32, just before my high school graduation, my dad bought a place on Eastman Street three blocks away in City Terrace. He had accumulated enough money from being in business, after the bank failed in '31, to buy a house in '32. There were all kinds of deals then. Because we had just come to Los Angeles, he didn't have a record of credit here, but the seller carried the loan so that he could make money from the interest. It was from Eastman Street that I married my wife Sadie. From there we knocked around between our parents' houses for a while before we got an apartment on Leward Street and before we went to San Francisco in '33 and '34.

Chapter 7: The Chicken Business

While we still lived on Blanchard Street in L.A., we bought a flat bed stake truck with a fourteen-foot bed and some cages, or chicken coops. My dad started buying and selling poultry: chickens, ducks, and turkeys. Perhaps it was because of his experience selling chickens in Atlantic City or perhaps because of the influence of his father who had traded in livestock. Little by little we had a nice living.

Stores that sold live chickens (there was no refrigeration) would keep them in chicken coops in the front of the store. When they sold one, they would take it back to the "killing room" and hang the chicken up and slit its throat, kosher style. There was sawdust on the floor.

My dad talked to different proprietors along Brooklyn Avenue who

My Father, Aaron Reznick

bought chickens along there. In those days you had chicken stores that only handled live chickens because there were a lot of religious Jews in the neighborhood who would only eat fresh-killed (Kosher) chickens. Pop thus discovered a market for live chickens; if he brought in live chickens from the country, the shopkeepers would buy them.

In the newspapers, even today, it lists the going price of commodities. Thus Dad knew he could, for example, get 12 cents a pound wholesale for live chickens. He would offer the farmer 9 cents a pound and deliver his chickens to market. If the farmer wanted more money than Dad could get back from the sale, he just wouldn't buy them. The farmer knows he's got to give up three cents to get his chickens delivered to market.

There was a lot of weight loss en route from one place to another. Dad had to go way out of town to find the chicken ranches. It was a good five-hour trip. He would travel to places like Hemet, Riverside, or San Bernardino; find the ranches and bring the chickens back to town. If he bought 1,000 pounds of chickens, when he got to town he would

Three Types of Chickens

There were three types of chickens: there was the common egg-laying hen; then there were fryers, the males, with a large body. In the "fryer club" a six-week old was pretty big, maybe twice as big as an egg layer. If the farmer raised chickens for food rather than eggs, he would sell them off at six weeks, because after six weeks they didn't gain very much if anything. Whereas the others, Rhode Island Reds, Plymouth Rocks, the egg laying chickens, were only replaced once or twice a year.

The second type of chicken farmer raised chickens strictly for food. He would sell the females to the egg-producing farmers. The males were raised as roasters, fryers and broilers. The males grew fast in the first six weeks and then they were ready for sale – young and easy to fry. The bigger ones, after six weeks, were roasters. The broiler is a much smaller chicken, maybe they're runts. In the first month you observe how they grow and classify them. The broiler you can broil all at once because they are smaller, turn it over once. After they reached this six week peak they didn't gain much weight but kept right on eating anyway.

A capon is a castrated rooster. The roosters didn't gain much weight because they were always running around fertilizing the chickens. You can tell a fertilized egg because there is a white spot next to the yolk. If you sit on it you are going to get a chicken. A capon just liked to lazy around and put on weight. A capon demanded a better price per pound. They had a better taste because they were fatter.

have 900 pounds of chickens due to the weight loss en route. He had to take all that into consideration when he made a bid for some chickens.

In his flat bed truck Pa carried twelve coops. Even though he had the truck serviced every Saturday, it still broke down now and then. There was no sign on the truck or anything.

There were two kinds of farmers, one that sold hens, who were in the egg business. The egg-producing hens would produce eggs for about five years, and then they would be old hens. The farmer would have one, two, three, four and five-year old hens. At some point the farmer would sell a batch of old and getting-older hens, maybe once or twice a year. My father would get to know when the farmers were ready to sell a batch of hens. There might be one, two or three truckloads of hens ready for sale. He might have to come back every day for a few days to haul the chickens into town because he could only take so many chickens in the coops at one time. He would lose some poultry on every trip; make a left or right turn and everybody loses their balance and they'd all be crushed into one corner and they stayed there! As a consequence one or two chickens were smothered. When you come home to deliver this stuff, you find a half a dozen dead chickens, in addition to the fact that they lose weight along the way.

Pop looks in the paper and it says that chicken is selling for 12 cents a pound, market price. The storekeeper also looks in the paper, and says well, I better charge 15, or whatever he decides to charge. Sometimes you lose, for example, if you bought the chickens for nine cents and the next day you go to sell them and the price is nine cents! On the other hand, if you bought the chickens for nine cents and the next day, you look in the paper, and the price is 14 cents, then you win! The market controls the prices.

One time my brother Manny was helping Pa out; they were hauling chickens from San Bernardino or Riverside and somehow the truck swerved and the live cargo tumbled out, with chickens running helter-skelter on the country road, and difficult to catch! The police were there and everyone was running around trying to catch chickens. I wasn't there. We were worried because they came home late.

The place on Eastman Street had a big yard. Pa built a chicken shack and added a garage. There was a kitchen and living room/dining room and two bedrooms along with a screened porch. After I got married and we stayed with the folks, Manny slept out on the screened porch. There was a side yard with banana trees and a loquat tree with delicious fruit which we enjoyed.

There were more chickens being sold at holidays: Christmas, Thanksgiving or Passover for example, and the price would generally go up because of the increase in demand. By storing them in the yard for opportune times of sale, Pa could pick up on the weight and also on the selling price of the poultry. I imagine he did pretty well, making a nice living doing that. After a while the farmers got to know him and trusted him in a good relationship. He had a buying source that was forthcoming all the time and he also had a dependable selling source. This was about 1931 until 1940.

Pa wasn't a formal businessman, with business cards and all that. If someone wanted his phone number, he would take a corner of the newspaper, rip it off, write his phone number on it, and give it to them. I don't ever remember him spending money on business cards. As a chicken peddler, five days a week Pa had workman's clothes on. In Europe he wore a suit, as an executive for the general. He wore a suit in the U.S. on holidays or when we went visiting to friends or relatives on the weekend. When he was working as a chicken peddler he wore jeans. If it were cold he would wear a leather jacket. He also had a sheepskin jacket, with the wool on the inside. In the summertime on weekends he would wear a suit without the jacket. He may not even have worn a vest; just the pants and a shirt. He may not have even been wearing a tie because it was too warm. It depended on the time of year and the occasion.

In 1935 Pa rented a store that was available on 4th Street and Anderson. It was like a garage with a lifting door where we sold live chickens and eggs like the other stores. This expanded Pa's ability to sell. If the other stores didn't want to buy the chickens he would just take them into his own store. If there were no room in the store he would put them in his yard. The area was called Russian Town. At that time there were not many native-born Californians. Immigrants were comfortable living among their own people, thus Russian Town. 4th Street was sort of a main drag but it was still residential. At that time you weren't too particular about zoning (e.g. residential, commercial). It was in an industrial section, mixed with residential. This was a Russian neighborhood with Russians who wanted chickens. The Russians were not as particular as the Kosher Jews. The process was simpler and my parents, of course, spoke Russian.

In one back corner of the store there were cages of live chickens. In the other back corner the chickens were killed, thrown in a barrel of sawdust and de-feathered in hot water which had been boiled in a big pot on a portable gas burner which plugged into a gas outlet. There was sawdust all over the floor. We would sweep it out as needed. It depended. For example, if it were raining, the customers took most of the sawdust with them on their wet shoes. It was pretty "garagey" looking. It wasn't even wood, just cement bricks.

Customers would come in and say "I want that chicken." I spoke Russian to them if they spoke Russian to me. If it were necessary, I could do it. My parents knew Russian but they hated Russia and didn't want to speak Russian at home. They spoke Yiddish or tried to speak English.

A customer would come in, look around, evaluate the chickens and say "I want that chicken." I would bring it out and they would feel the chicken's bottom to see how fat it was. If they wanted chicken fat (called schmaltz, which was kosher; lard was not) for cooking for example, they might like a fat chicken. A nice big fat old chicken would also be good to stuff (bigger cavity) and roast. A smaller chicken, a fryer, a male chicken, with less fat and less bulk, would go well in the frying pan. The customer would select their chicken and then I would weigh it and if they wanted it killed I would take it in the back and kill it in a modified kosher manner with a sharp razor; slit the throat in other words. In the Kosher manner the windpipe is not cut, and the manner of death is painless. However, I didn't know about not cutting the windpipe because I wasn't a trained to be a kosher butcher and neither was my father. We probably did cut the windpipe. I didn't say any prayer. The Hebrew prayer was, "Thank you God for providing us with our daily food." We had a whetstone to sharpen the knife. If I felt it was dull I would do that. Then I would throw the chicken in the barrel loaded with sawdust where it would bleed to death in a relatively painless manner. (We didn't want to administer a lot of pain to the damn chickens!) The chicken would thrash around a bit for about three minutes and then keel over dead. I would then put it in the hot (not boiling) water for about 30 seconds. The water wasn't boiling because we didn't want to cook the chicken! Also, I was involved and didn't want to burn my hand! The hot water would get in between the feathers and loosen them up. I would then hold up the chicken by its legs and run my hands over it to remove the feathers, which came off easily, in about a minute.

Ma would run the store while Pa bought and sold chickens. I would help out in the store and on the routes. The store was a bit of a drive from the folk's house. By this time I was older and had married. For helping him when I could Pa would give me a chicken and a dozen eggs, which I appreciated very much. Later, I would also pitch in money to the folks from what I made on my own with the Examiner and such. As a member of the family, you help out. When we were first married, Sadie and I lived with the folks off and on. I realized early that the chicken business would not support two families.

We had a sign outside the door which said "InterNat" for "International Poultry Company". The Russians were there, so that's international. Manny liked that name. Manny, after going to college wanted Pa to expand the business but my father didn't want to do that. He felt he couldn't control it. Manny was very disappointed. There was a wholesale company called Young's and Manny used that as an example that you can get bigger and more well-known. Manny looked for my support, which I gave. Everyone is eating chicken these days. It's better for you than beef and cheaper. I think sometimes, "Where would we be today if we had expanded like Manny wanted?" Nothing came of it.

Chapter 8: College or Not

Pa had wanted me to go to college and had saved money for this purpose, depositing it in the U.S. Bank, probably on Brooklyn Ave. That bank went broke during the Depression in '31. There was no money. I'm not talking about $25, I'm talking about several hundred dollars; to save several hundred dollars when my father was trying to get us out of the hole there...he was the one that saved the money. I had no ability to save that kind of money. Now that money was gone. Years later, when it was finally settled, he got ten cents on the dollar. In the meantime Pa went to work and started all over again and it

High School Photo

High School Graduation

was hard enough to make enough money for his family let alone save money for my college education.

I graduated from high school in '32. The college prep high school education was always good. It gave you a pretty broad knowledge of what's going on in the world. My college money was gone and saving money takes time. If I started saving money to go to college when I graduated, I would be 25 when I started going to college and there was no guarantee that I would have the money then. It wouldn't have been a good plan. It was just too far down the line. That's your choice; you either go to college or you get a job. Well, okay, I'll get a job, under these circumstances. That was the solution. I guess I was disappointed because I would have preferred to go to college but don't forget, this was '31 and I was still in school. The bank closed in '31. I graduated in '32. By then it was no longer an issue. I still finished my high school. I just didn't go to college. A year after the loss this was a foregone conclusion so it didn't matter.

My brother Manny graduated from high school in '36 and went to college in '37, graduating in '41 from the University of California, Berkeley, cum laude with a Phi Beta Kappa. We were all very proud. When Manny graduated he went to my father and asked for the gold watch my father had promised him when he graduated.

Manny was never very interested in school as a kid. He went from a "C" student to winning a scholarship and graduating Phi Beta Kappa from the University of California in Berkeley. I had already been married for three years. I was surprised when Manny started getting "A's" in high school. I've never seen anybody do such a turn around as Manny did. He had a friend in the last couple of years of high school in the same grade, who was an all "A" student, who had a tremendous influence on him. He said "What are you wasting your time for? Why don't you study more?" They were very close friends for a long time. When Manny went to college, we grew closer together because the age difference began to be more insignificant. When we were younger Manny always wanted to be with me and I was really too much older.

Chapter 9: Sadie

I met Sadie in eleventh grade when we came to Los Angeles. My first meeting with Sadie was significant and foreshadowed our future together. Her boyfriend, Sam, lived across the hall from my Aunt Celia where we were staying when we first came to L.A. He brought me to school and we were friends thereafter. Sam was a year and a half older than I, Jewish, slender with blond hair. Sam dressed nicely. I dressed as nicely as I could. Sam had a scar on top of his head where he didn't have hair. He combed it over and it didn't look that bad.

We were going up the stairs to class at Roosevelt High in Boyle Heights and he saw Sadie entering a classroom, crossing the hall, maybe 50 feet away. He yelled "Hi!" and she waited for him. He told me to wait there for him. Meanwhile she's looking at me and I'm looking at her and we kind of smiled at each other. What he did was sort of unusual. Instead of saying "Hey, come on I want you to meet my girlfriend," he tells me, "Stay there!" as though he had a premonition. Anyway, he chatted with her for a few minutes and came back to get me and to continue where we were going.

This was the beginning of December. I had just arrived a day or two before to California. After a week or so I knew most of the kids in my classes. I kept getting introductions through Sam. About a week before New Year's Eve a girl came up to Sam. I was also standing there; she invited Sam and Sadie to a New Year's Eve party at her house. Sam introduced me. She said "I'm glad to meet you" and, "How about you coming too?" I said, "Okay."

I was still at my aunt's house. Sam knocks on my door, after dinner and says "Let's go." We went to his car, a Buick. Sam was about five foot nine, taller than I was. We're both wearing suits with ties and everything. I was wearing the same suit I later wore for my graduation and picture. We were juniors in high school and I had been in town about two weeks. We went to pick up Sadie. She wasn't dressed elaborately. She was just a girl at that point. She didn't mean anything to me. She came down the steps at her house on Pomeroy, City Terrace. So he got out of the car and helped her into the passenger side of the front seat by opening the door and introduced her to me. Of course I remembered the previous incident where he hadn't introduced us, which sort of engendered a curiosity. He had to introduce me to her now because I was sitting in the back seat. The party was off Brooklyn Ave, more central than City Terrace.

After the party really got going, there were about twenty-five or thirty people there. They had picked up the rug in the living room/dining room area so that you could dance. They played music on the record player, the music of the day, 1931: fox trot, waltz, Charleston. There were cokes, pretzels, cookies and stuff like that around on the table. The parents weren't in view. They wanted us to have the freedom of not being watched or they might have gone to another party.

I didn't know anyone. Having been introduced to Sadie, and since Sam had been asked to dance by some other girl, I asked Sadie to dance and we started dancing. There seemed to be some sort of magnetic situation between us. From there on in every time Sam danced with somebody else, I would dance with Sadie. She would come up to me or I would go up to her. I danced with her more than anybody else. Pretty soon we were laughing together. She had a sense of humor. It was sort of a deep sense of humor. It wasn't something practiced, something she remembered. It wasn't a matter of having a bunch of jokes. Sadie did not have a repertoire. Her sense of humor was spontaneous. We were no longer stiff with each other. By the time it was over, I must have danced with her ten or twelve times. A lot of boys asked her to dance but she said she already had a dance. In other words, she danced with me as much as she could. After the dance she would stay with me until the next one started.

Sam knew everybody and he would dance with Sadie, but he would dance with everyone else also. Usually you had an escort and you would dance with him maybe five times and another ten times you would dance with other people. But Sadie stayed by me because she wanted to dance with me. Maybe I was a good dancer and the other guys weren't.

The party lasted until about 1:00 a.m. Then they served some stuff. There were too many people to sit down so you walked around. At midnight we sang Auld Lang Syne. It was nice that I was able to be included in something after such a short period of time. I suppose I'm kind of a friendly guy. After that evening Sadie and I were no longer strangers.

I felt uncomfortable because I didn't want to offend Sam but that's the way it went and Sam did not seem to mind. We were friends, going to school together. Sam had the car or he didn't. Sometimes we would pick Sadie up and walk with her or she would come by and we would walk to school. Sam had two very good friends, Leo and Dave, and I was becoming the fourth friend. Sam's parents had money. His father and his uncle owned a company called Advance Furniture Company. They might have had a contract with Sears to make certain items. Later on he worked for his father, and when his father died

With Sadie in 1931

he became the owner and he got a contract to make furniture exclusively for Sears. Sam drove a big Buick. Sam wasn't affected by the Depression as much as other people.

There was a company that had a lot of stores that sold real thick milk shakes; a soda fountain. There was one not very far in Monterey Park and in Alhambra. They were popular with high school kids. Sam had a Buick and Leo had a Model T Ford. We would pile into it, including Sadie and Dave's girl friend. We would go to Alhambra and get a milk shake on the weekend, usually around one o'clock. One of our friends was an usher at a movie house and he would let us in free. Sadie was a member of the group.

As the year progressed Sadie and I ran into each other quite often, having one or two classes together. One Friday afternoon in late spring I told Sadie in a casual conversation I was going to take my Dad's car, the blue Plymouth, up to be serviced. I said "You want to come along?" She said, "Yeah, I'd like that." I got home, got the car, picked her up and a block before we got to the station, who should be walking down the street but Sam and his friends. I hadn't yet reached the level of equality as far as the other three were concerned. As far as I was concerned, Sadie and I were friends. I waved to the guys and they waved back, a little reluctantly. Except that back at school they don't talk to Sadie or me. The incident threw us together in such a way that she and Sam were no longer a couple. Also, I had been becoming a part of a group of Sam's friends but because of this I was not. So Sadie and I, thrown together as it were, started seeing each other more. I was sorry to lose Sam as a friend but that was the way it went. Later in life we became friends again.

Sadie and I started walking to school together. I knew when she would be at the corner and I waited for her. We made arrangements. After school the same thing. I carried her books. It didn't take very long after we were abandoned by Sam and Leo and Dave that we started going together. On Saturdays we would go to the movies at the Wabash Theatre in City Terrace. It cost ten cents. You got a candy bar too. There wasn't that much sexuality about it. We went out together. It was the end of our junior year in high school. We spent the summer and our senior year in high school getting to know each other. This was 1931.

When Sadie and I started going steady we would go to each other's houses and we would sit on the couch. Her father and mother used to go out on Saturday, downtown to a show or whatever. Sadie's sisters and brother would also go out. On Saturday afternoon it was just the two of us and we would stay at home and neck. She used the same rules as the girls in Atlantic City, as all girls did then. We did a lot of kissing and a lot of feeling of the breasts and that was it. Of course there were some girls of the same age who let the rules go by. It was never a secret. The boys would talk that so and so "put out." If you wanted to take advantage of the situation you could try. Maybe they turned you down or maybe they didn't.

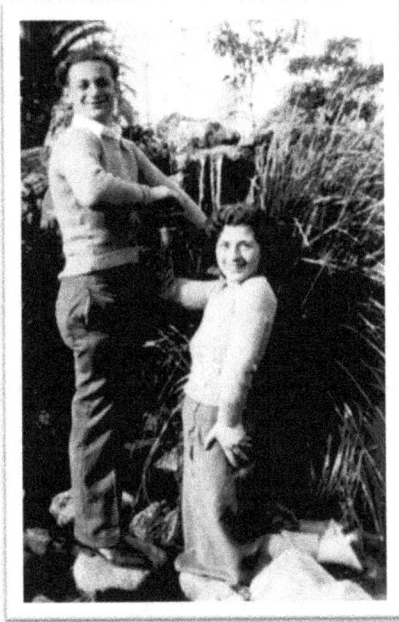

With Sadie in 1932

Sadie was straightforward that she would certainly not allow anything to happen. Maybe that's one of the reasons why we married as early as we did, because she wanted to go further but not unless we were married. As far as I was concerned, I pretty much felt the same way. I wanted her bad enough to marry her. We graduated from high school in June and got married the following February, eight months later. During that time her family moved to Mansfield Street in West L.A. It was hard to get up there and we couldn't see each other as often. I would see her on weekends and we would go for milk shakes.

With the girls in Atlantic City the situation was pre-determined that we weren't in love, but were going to experiment with being a man and a woman. It reduced your inquisitiveness, or whatever it was. I was more inquisitive because I didn't have any sisters.

With Sadie it was a different situation. We were in love before we started necking. We were thrown together and we started talking. We talked about whatever came up. I would classify Sadie's sister Bitzy as being somewhat of an "intellectual." She liked classical music. She liked opera. She liked the philharmonic orchestra and she would take Sadie there. So Sadie was exposed to this kind of stuff. I wasn't. So she began to expose me to it.

There were plays at the Biltmore Theatre; it was part of the Biltmore Hotel. One of the tricks was that if I got down there early, I could get a job as an usher. They didn't pay me but they allowed me to stay and see the show. It was just a one night job. I offered my services in return for seeing the stage play. It was an available situation, but you had to get there before somebody else did. The first 20 guys got the job. After that you were too late.

She would buy the ticket and I would get the job, and I would sit with her. Noel Coward was a popular writer back then. We saw his plays. So Sadie dragged me into a higher level of society than I was, although my mother was pretty much like that. My mother did a lot of reading. My father was intelligent and intellectual but he rarely put me into a situation where I would learn something about music or whatever. At one point he got me a violin. I think I took about five lessons and I quit. The teacher told my father that I should quit because I just did not have the talent! I was maybe 11 or 12.

I remember I took Sadie to the Cotton Club in Culver City on Saturday night to celebrate our high school graduation. It was the thing to do. This was a nice place, not cheap. In those days five dollars for two people was a lot of money. There was a doorman in uniform. Inside was a nice big room with a dance floor. The tables where you had your dinner were in a raised area, one step higher all the way around the dance floor. The orchestra was at one end of the dance floor. This was in 1932. The band was always famous, like Tommy Dorsey or his brother, Jimmy. There were five or six players: enough music to dance to. Always drums, a piano and saxophone; maybe a guitar or a clarinet or a trumpet.

We were double dating with some friends. For some reason I couldn't take my dad's Plymouth so we made arrangements to go with Billy Sorenson, who had a car, and his girlfriend. It was a good deal: drinks, chicken with all the trimmings, desert, a show; all for $5.00. One of my classes in high school was photography. All my friends used to come to me to develop their stuff after class. For 2 cents I sold them their pictures. At first it was just a favor. There was a lot of demand. I would buy the paper from the school. I used the developing solution which was good for 24 hours and was going to be thrown out. If my friends went to Thrifty Drugstore it cost them 5 cents. So I had money. At the end of the meal I pulled out my bag of change which I had from emptying out my piggy bank. Sadie and the others were very embarrassed! She asked me on the way home, "Couldn't you have gone to the bank?" Well, I wasn't about to go the bank which had closed and lost all the money my dad had saved for my college education! To me it didn't make any difference; I hadn't given it much thought. I had no sophistication at all. Later I got etiquette education from Sadie.

After we got out of the Cotton Club it was probably midnight and we were supposed to have a good time all night long so we drove around and got home around three o'clock in the morning without much happening except a little necking here and there.

Sadie read a lot of the current stuff. She also liked classic stuff like Little Women or Charles Dickens' Oliver. During the early period of our relationship, my mother liked Sadie very much. But later, my mother resented the fact that Sadie and I ran off to get married and lied to them about it. The Depression was on and I didn't want to put a burden on her parents. We would have had to have a grand celebration and they wouldn't have let us get married at eighteen. They would have talked us out of it. They would have said, "Look, you haven't even got a job. You do this. You do that."

Chapter 10: A Secret Plan

I graduated from high school in 1932 which was the depth of the Depression. Nobody was a rich person. And yet, everyone who graduated in my class, maybe 30 people, was very successful in later years, like Sam and the furniture company. He developed it beyond his father's level. I worked in the Post Office and went into the Mail Delivery business. We had reunions with the graduates of '32. Most of the graduates attended. You found out how they're doing. One of them became an agent for Chevrolet. He became a rich man selling Chevys. He owned the agency.

Ultimately a vacancy opened up at a supermarket owned by the boxer Jesse Willard, (who was beaten by Jack Dempsey). Jesse opened up the first supermarket, in the United States as far as I know, on Fountain and Vine. It had a grocery department, and a butcher, and it had a deli. I had a friend, Shy, was working at the deli and he got me a job there also. In fact, he used to pick me up and we'd go to work together. I ended up really learning a lot about the deli business.

We had to work six days and we got $13.00 a week. We would go early in the morning and make up the salad items, like potato salad or coleslaw which were made every morning. Sometimes there were leftovers and the employees could take them home because the food had to be freshly prepared every day. In the morning you would try to estimate how much you would need. Sometimes you ran out, sometimes you didn't. There was a pecking order. Most of the time, the manager took all the leftovers. Once in a while he would say "Hey, you guys need any stuff?" I worked at the deli through the summer of '32, after my high school graduation.

Another friend, Bernie Pleet, told me he was working for Jack Perlman at Hearst Newspapers and making $20 - $25 a week. If I could make more money, I could get married, although I didn't think it through that way. I went to work for Jack and made more money. He was glad to hire me, it didn't cost him anything! Whereas at the deli I was making $13 a week; selling subscriptions I made $25. Once in a while I would hit a streak and make $100! I was selling Examiner subscriptions, living at home on Eastman Street. I didn't have my own car. I used my thumb all over the place.

However, my dad had the old Plymouth and that wasn't being used so I took it to the office I worked out of, on Eleventh between Broadway and Main, the main office for the Examiner. We used to park in a "No Parking Zone" because we knew the policeman. The policeman was very friendly with us and he knew we worked there and so he didn't bother giving us any tickets. But every now and then he was off, and we'd get a ticket. We argued but the policeman said "I'm sorry, the ticket's already out, I can't tear it up." And then we found out that if you got a ticket and the policeman didn't show up at court, nothing happened. We found out later because we showed up and he didn't, deliberately, because he didn't want to hurt us; he was just following normal procedure. Even so, there were two or three times that we had to pay the ticket. In those days, a ticket was maybe ten dollars, which was a lot of money.

One weekend afternoon in January we were home alone, just the two of us. Sadie was working as a county clerk. I was selling subscriptions for the Examiner newspaper and we were both living at home. We were lying down in front of the fireplace at her folks' with the fire burning. In those days you didn't have any money to spend. We spent a lot of time by ourselves when we could because it was nice to do. We were watching the fire, talking in general and the subject of marriage came up. There was no sexuality involved except kissing, but we were hoping there could be.

I don't know who brought the subject up. It could have been me because I felt that I had a job and was learning the business, so to speak. We both wanted each other but the rules were pretty strict and it wasn't going to happen any other way. I figured "Well, I'm earning a living. Two could live as cheaply as one." That's what they said. It's not true, but it's almost true. Rent is the same for two as it is for one.

Most of my money at that time was donated to my parents because they needed the money. When we were lying down there we decided to get married right away. Before, it was planning for the future. It was a foregone conclusion. As long as we had both our health, we didn't have to worry about excessive expenditures. If we got married, we would have the satisfaction of being together all the time. We could play house. Sadie was a good cook. She would provide the meals and I would provide the money to get the meals. The decision was made to get married. There was no money for college and we wanted to marry. You look at the situation and you come to a conclusion and that's it. Forget about college; go on with your life without going to college. The whole plan would have been different without the Depression. I probably wouldn't even have gotten married at that point. Being a practical individual, I could have said, "There's no point in being married. We can still be sweethearts and you wait until I get out of college and then we'll get married." Under the circumstances, going to college was no longer an option. The idea of saving money was always there. The point is that there wasn't enough money to save. How much money can you save on $13 a week? We tried to save money living with our parents but that didn't work out because it was hard for them. They were in the Depression too. When we graduated I looked around for a job but it was always temporary. They always used you. If they had a son in there and the son went on vacation they hired you without telling you that the son was coming back.

So Sadie and I decided to marry. We told a couple of lies. We were going steady to such a degree that I could tell my folks that I was going to sleep over at Sadie's. Her family had moved from City Terrace to West L.A., to us quite a distance. I told my folks that I was going to sleep over at her house and she told her folks that she was going to sleep over at my house. Instead, we went with a friend of ours, someone for whom I worked, Jack Perlman, who was about 10 years older, who took us to Oxnard where we got married by a Justice of the Peace. Jack sort of encouraged us. He was the first to know about our decision. He said, if you want to elope, I'll take you. He had married young also. Jack knew that if we married locally it would appear in the newspapers under "statistics" and so we would have to leave town.

Sadie and I met at Jack's place. We left for Oxnard with Jack and his wife in the late afternoon. When we got there we went to a Justice of the Peace, at his house, around 10:30 p.m. Jack had found out ahead of time where he lived and he took me the day before to Ventura to get the license. We knocked on his door. The justice opened up the window upstairs, said "Who's there?" with his night gown and sleeping hat. He said, "Okay, I'll be right down." He married us in his night gown, just like in the movies. His wife was there too as a witness. It was a quick thing. He was going back to bed. We went into his living room. He looked over our papers, said "Okay, stand over here" and performed the ceremony and then said, "two dollars please." And we were married! Sadie had gone to the dime store and bought a twenty-five cent ring, but it looked like a wedding ring. She never threw it away and wore it for a long time. We lied about our age. You couldn't get married under twenty-one without parental consent. He didn't ask for anything except the two dollars.

After our marriage, in February of '33, we stayed at Jack's place overnight, on West Jefferson. He had a nice apartment with two bedrooms. We had a nice breakfast with them; probably bacon and eggs, and then we went back to our respective homes, not saying anything.

We were going to keep it a secret but our folks happened to meet each other the following week. My mother commented to Sadie's mother that she hoped I wasn't a nuisance. Her mother said, "What do you mean, I should be telling you that I hoped Sadie wasn't a nuisance!" Then they found out that we didn't stay at each other's houses. They confronted us with this information and the secret of the elopement went down the drain. Our parents probably got together and decided that since they couldn't do anything about it they might as well be positive about it.

Sadie's father insisted that we have another ceremony in which we would be married by a rabbi. A week or so after we eloped, we were re-married on March 11, 1933, in the Jewish tradition. It was the middle of the Depression. The Jewish ceremony is like the civil ceremony except that there are some traditions. It was something her parents wanted, so we did it.

At the Jewish ceremony, Sadie and I got married under a huppa, a little square cloth roof held up by four poles. The huppa was in the house. When you finalize the marriage you break a glass. They put a glass inside a napkin and the groom stamps it to break the glass. It symbolizes the breaking of the bad stuff around and now there is a clear path. There's some traditional wine in the ceremony, given to you in a single silver engraved cup. The groom takes a sip and then the bride takes a sip.

Wedding Day

We invited some friends to the wedding at Sadie's parents' home, with a little party afterward. It was around 3 o'clock in the afternoon, about three weeks after our elopement. We lived at our respective houses meanwhile.

There was some booze and everybody had a shot. I don't remember any presents. It was in the middle of very hard times, the

Depression. They kept saying "Two can live as cheaply as one." When we were first married in Oxnard, I was 18; at the second wedding I was 19. My birthday was March the 3rd and we were married again on March 11th. The first wedding was February 25th. Sadie was three months younger.

Her whole family was at the wedding along with my family. Some of her friends and some of my friends were there. Jack Perlman came and some of the guys I was working with. Not a lot of people. While we were getting married the house was shaking from an aftershock of the earthquake of '33. I don't remember any kind of a party but there must have been some whiskey there, you know, to offer a drink for a l'chaim. The wedding was performed at 11:00 a.m. I was wearing a suit that I had. I don't remember much after that. The earth was still quaking. The aftershocks were going on for a long time, a couple of weeks afterward.

I figured I could make it all right. In those days, you just gambled; you just jumped into it.

Bertalon Marton, Sadie's father, and Elsa, Sadie's mother, came to the US in about 1911 from Hungary. They came about the same time my mother's folks came but they stayed. Things were peaceful until 1914, when the war broke out. Two of her sisters were born in Hungary. Her sister Mae was born in 1912 in Cleveland. Sadie was born in 1914 in Cleveland also. When she was 4, they moved to Denver. Then they came to Los Angeles when she was about 5, before us,

Sadie's Parents in Hungary

about 1919. Sadie's family lived off of Brooklyn Avenue in Boyle Heights and then moved to Pomeroy in City Terrace, to a big house.

Neither Sadie's parents nor my parents had a college education, but the men were educated through the chaider arm of the synagogue. Sadie's mother's father had been a rabbi in Hungary. Number one on the list was education. They realized that without education you had no chance at all. Hungary was much more liberal than Russia. The Jews were allowed to live in the cities. There was more culture, more art, in the city as compared to the country where my parents were, "somewhere around Kiev.' Sadie had class. She had artistic taste. Her parents came from Budapest. Her father might have been a tailor over there.

Sadie's father was a religious man. He looked like Groucho Marx and had a sense of humor. He was a nice man. His business went to pot because of the Depression and it affected him so bad that he ultimately died. They had moved uptown to a duplex, but it was really maintained by their daughters. The daughters wanted them to be in a better neighborhood. Boyle Heights was deteriorating. The Martons always wanted to maintain a nice front. Bitsy and Mae and Betty were there and Jerry who went to L.A. High, and Sadie. It had a nice porch and a nice living room.

Sadie's father was a designer in the garment business and prior to 1929, he made

The Grandparents on Marvin's first Birthday

a lot of money. But he didn't save it, he would spend it. He bought a big car, a Studebaker, and stuff like that. They did a lot of partying and vacationing. They would go to Elsinore and Murietta Hot Springs a lot. In fact, they used to take me and Sadie along with them. It included meals and so wasn't too expensive, considering how it was. They would go there even in bad times.

I was not religious. I never was. But, for practical purposes, it's easier to marry within your own group. Then, in the heat of an argument, one person doesn't end up saying something like, "You dirty Jew!" It's one less burden. My parents were from different geographic locations, but they were both Jewish.

Chapter 11: Married Life

We were married in 1933. At that time, Sadie's parents' house was a comparatively new, more modern house; very nice: a duplex in the West End off La Brea and Mansfield. They lived upstairs. There were outside stairs to the second residence. Sadie was one of six children, with four sisters and one brother. Sadie's sister, Bitzy, was working and lived there. She was not married. Jerry was also living there and bringing in money. Bitzy and Mae and Nellie were all bringing in money when they all lived on Pomeroy in City Terrace.

Mr. Marton was a women's clothing designer of what were called "women's play clothes." They were summer clothes. Clothing design is a good business except that during the Depression everyone wore last year's styles. Around '35 or '36, Sadie's father went broke. He had a lot of goods that he had designed and manufactured but nobody would buy them. He had invested a lot of money in merchandise and he had a loft down on Los Angeles Street and he had a factory there. He was a very good designer but his clothes weren't practical for people who didn't have the money. If they had money, they would buy dresses, not sportswear.

People cancelled their orders. He wound up with a bunch of stuff he couldn't sell. He had invested his money in it and now all of a sudden he didn't have the money to pay for rent. I had my own problems at the time and wasn't privy to their family discussions. By that time I had a baby and was working at the Post Office. I was still an outsider. Their money problems "weren't my business." Ultimately it became my business because I had to pony up some money in order to get some of his debts taken care of. Everybody had to chip in for the lawyer to get the thing straightened out. His son Jerry, who was an accountant, tried to bail him out but he couldn't. Mr. Marton was also involved with his son-in-law Chuck who, through college, had also learned to be an accountant. He had these two money managers trying to figure out how to handle this thing. But whoever he owed money to, he never paid them because he never had the money. Working in the Post Office on a part-time basis wasn't very productive so I couldn't really afford much. But now I was a member of the family.

As a matter of fact, the whole thing was so bad for him that he got sick. He just never recovered. He died when he was fifty-five years old, in '42, just after the war started. He was a very nice man. I liked him. I was at work and I got a phone call. I went to the phone and Sadie told me that her father had died. In later years, when her mother was living in a senior citizen's home, we all contributed toward it; 20 to 25 dollars a month.

Sadie's father was funny. He was always part of the conversation, a welcome addition to any conversation. Before the Depression, he could afford to be a big spender. Sadie's mother was a very nice lady. She was a "mother." She was a good cook. She did the cleaning. She took care of them when they were sick — that type of thing. I don't remember her discussing politics or anything "serious." My mother was more involved in world affairs than her mother was. When you talked to her mother, she would talk to you about her food, how to make food, how to do this or how to do that. It was always confined to family affairs. Sadie got all of her worldliness from her sister Bitzy.

After we were married Sadie didn't work. She had been working at the county about six months and they were laying people off like everybody else and she didn't have any kind of seniority. Sadie's eldest sister was Nellie, who married Harry Wolf a couple of years before we married. He worked in draperies at the Columbia studios. Then came Bitzy (Elizabeth), who worked as a secretary in a wholesale grocery company and later married Jay Etkin. Next was Mae, who had been going with Chuck Strahl in high school and was sort of already engaged to him. Then came Sadie, then Jerry, then Betty, the youngest. All of Sadie's sisters married Jewish men.

When I married Sadie I married into a big family which gave me a lot of connections. Every weekend we would get together for picnics at Roxbury Park in the winter time, or go to the beach in the summertime. In the thirties and forties there was no television. The Depression was on. There was association with other people. You had closer relationships with your relatives. With Sadie's relatives there were six men and six women in the group. Every Sunday in the winter, if it rained, the men stayed in and played poker. We played a lot of poker together. At the beach in the summer we would throw balls or whatever. It was always an association with your relatives.

On my side I had one brother who was not around. On her side she had four sisters and a brother, all of whom were around. The friendships and relationships were on her side, not on mine. Our outings with Sadie's relatives lasted until the war started in '39, about six years. We kept up with them over the years. They're our friends. We had some other friends and we played poker with them too. Most of them were from high school. We had fun: Picnics and cookouts at the beach for example.

Right after we were married by the rabbi we went to live with my folks for a short time in East Los Angeles on Eastman. We had the bedroom. We were there for a month or two. There was a lack of privacy, however, when you needed it most. We decided to move. We found this place in central Los Angeles on Leward between 7th and

Wilshire, downtown. It was furnished. We didn't need anything to move in except personal things like clothes.

I went to San Francisco to sell newspaper subscriptions soon after we were married and stayed about two months in a hotel downtown. Later I got an apartment on Eddy Street in San Francisco. I paid $30 for a month's rent, including utilities; everything but a phone. It was also furnished. I sent Sadie $25 and told her to come up, by boat. She came up with one suitcase. It was a single apartment. Most single apartments at that time had what they called "Murphy beds." It's fancy-looking on the outside but when you pull it down it's really a bed. However, we shoved a bed in the walk-in closet and we could hardly get into bed but that's what we did. Our first apartment on Leeward in Los Angeles had a Murphy bed. Otherwise, it was like a living room. No bedroom. The next tier was with a bedroom, and the tier after that was with two bedrooms.

The San Francisco apartment was nice. It had a kitchen. They're not very large places. There was a hallway at the entry which probably had a closet. Sadie became friends with Lorna, who was the wife of one of my workmates, Ben.

Sadie with Barbara, 1941

At that time, we had walkathons. It was a dancing situation, dancing to records, where there were contestants and there were winners. For two or three days you schlep each other around. This was continuous. No sleep, no nothing. I don't know how they stood it. So you went there at night and it cost a quarter to get in there. We would go and pick a favorite and so did everybody else. We showed our support by clapping and yelling for them. It went on until all but one couple dropped out. Those things usually lasted a week. The winners got money.

We went to the theatre a lot because we lived downtown. There was a big movie house, the Orpheum. They had vaudeville acts before the movie. Some of the big stars started with vaudeville, like the Nicholas Brothers. They were probably the best tap dancers that ever lived. There were two brothers. One of them was maybe 5'10" and the other was about 4' because he was only twelve years old. They danced with precision. Later they were the same height; maybe ten years apart.

The vaudeville was on two or three times a day and the movies were three or four times a day. They kept on repeating. That was fun and it wasn't too expensive so we were able to afford it, so we had a good time in San Francisco.

We ate out a lot too, and they had some great restaurants. They weren't that expensive in those days. One of our favorites was a coffee shop. It was open 24 hours a day and most of the seating was at the bar, where the cooks were on the other side. The fun part was watching these cooks cook. They'd throw things around. They would throw knives up in the air and they'd fry eggs and the eggs would go way up in the air and turn around. So it was a lot of entertainment in the food, and the food was good, mostly Italian. Sadie and I would get a couple of seats in front of our favorite cook, because we ate there very often. They may still be there! I remember there was a deli on Van Ness that we enjoyed. We always liked to go to the Wharf in San Francisco. We would look at the crabs and then eat them at the restaurant. We had as much fun as we could get. Don't waste your time – have fun!

A man doesn't need experience to be a father. Your wife has a baby. Suddenly you're a father. "What do I do?" Well, you play with the kid. Sometimes they enjoy it. Sometimes they don't. I used to throw them up in the air and catch them and they loved it. Nevertheless, what else can you do? You can talk to them, but even today I find it very difficult with my grandchildren and great grandchildren. It's easy with grownups because you find interests that you share and you can talk about it. I'm not particularly athletic. Many parents use sports as a way to bond.

"How's school?" What subject can you find? Sometimes you're being courteous by saying "How's school?", but you really don't care.

People go their own way, especially your own children, and you get together on special occasions. In spite of the fact that you let them go, at least they have the feeling that the parents are looking out for them, without interfering.

As a parent, you try to raise good kids. You try to see to it that they're honest and fair and good citizens. For example, when Marvin was about 12 years old, he was selling newspapers on the corner of Wilshire and La Brea. There was a drug store there. One day he comes home before dinner, very proud of himself, that he was honest and a good citizen. It seemed that he found a five dollar bill on the street. He went into the drug store waving the bill, asking, "Did anybody lose a five dollar bill." He had two or three volunteers, but he let them decide, giving it to them. He told us what happened when he got home. Obviously, he was taken advantage of. I got mad at him for being stupid but that's not fair to even say that. I was upset because he was being taken advantage of. It might have been that the owner of the five dollar bill had taken the bus and was long gone.

It takes wisdom to determine how to project to children that there are exceptions to the rule. The new rules begin to complicate things. A child doesn't have the ability to distinguish philosophical differences. Marvin was expecting great kudos from me and was bewildered that I was upset. It's hard to explain things nicely when you're upset.

The point being is that even though the kids are independent, they still know that you're there in case they need you.

In later years I bought Sadie a three and a half carat diamond. It was a perfect diamond, a perfectly clear white diamond, without a flaw. When we were in Japan, we met a woman from Poland who wound up in Tokyo, because of World War II, selling pearls. When we went there, having been told about her from Dora, we went to her and bought some pearls. We were also talking about diamonds and she gave me the name of a cousin who had a diamond business in New York, on 47th Street. That's the diamond center. The next time I was there, we looked them up and I told them that their cousin in Tokyo had sent us.

They showed us a diamond and said we could have it for 8 thousand. He said, you can take the diamond to Tiffany's or anywhere else and have it appraised, which we did. It was appraised at 25 thousand so I bought it. We had it mounted and she had this beautiful ring. Now it's worth about 50 thousand. The problem is that you can't wear it. It can be stolen! You could lose your life over the damn thing. So, what do you do? You put it away in the safe and you wear an ordinary ring. These are the crazy things of life. I wanted her to have something good. This was my wife, I loved her and this is what she liked. She talked about buying a diamond. If that's what she wanted, then she should have it. I was surprised at what jewelry she had because she very often bought it without me. One of the things she did when she was 65 and started drawing social security was open an account in her own name. She felt it was her money to do with as she pleased. In consequence, she bought a lot of stuff that I had no idea she had bought.

Sadie also liked to collect art. She picked the pictures and she had a very good eye. She picked one picture for $250 by a Argentinean artist, Aldo Luongo. She was keeping busy while I worked and was in Sherman Oaks walking along Ventura Blvd. and stopped in a gallery. The gallery salesman, probably the owner was impressed with her and said, "You can take it with you. If you like the picture, keep it. It's $250. If you don't like it, bring it back." Sadie liked art depicting lovers.

For example we have a Lladro sculpture in our bedroom depicting two Eskimos in a moment of personal affection. She liked the Luongo; so did everybody else. I gave it to Marvin. Today it's worth $24,000. After we had a lot of art, she would buy for other people.

One time we were in Paris and Charlie Mesnick had an introduction to one of the galleries. We went there and the proprietor invited us to dinner. After dinner he opened the shop and showed us around. There was this picture by Salvador Dali entitled "The Three Muses." It struck me as a beautiful rendition of the female aspect, and made me think of how practical it was; what a great invention! Sadie took note of my comments and without my knowledge she bought the picture. When we got home she unveiled it for my birthday. I don't even know what she paid for it. I was surprised and overwhelmed. I was stunned.

The Dali painting depicts the three goddesses, Hera, the goddess of power; Aphrodite, the goddess of love and Athena, the goddess of wisdom. Zeus asks Paris, a most handsome man, to choose the most beautiful of the three. Hera offers him all of Asia Minor. Athena offers supreme wisdom and Aphrodite offers him the most beautiful woman in the world. Paris picks Aphrodite as the most beautiful goddess for the gift she offers.

With Sadie in 1967

Helen of Sparta is the most beautiful woman and Paris sails to get her. This begins the Trojan War. The painting is of the three undraped goddesses, with a man's head (Paris) in there somewhere. I enjoyed comparing Salvador Dali's depiction of the three muses with famous renditions by other artists.

We had a fun anniversary party on our 40th. We had a reverse surprise party. We surprised our guests by putting them on a bus and we took them to the Queen Mary, where we had our party. They had a very nice restaurant up there; it was more like a nightclub. There was a singer and a dance floor with a band. It was the same sort of thing as the "Cotton Club" but more sophisticated. I didn't use my "piggy bank" to pay for it. By then money didn't bother me because I had it. I had been in business twenty years. It must have cost five thousand dollars. We invited all our friends. The bus held 49 people. We invited enough to get on the bus.

We took a two-week auto touring trip to Mexico for our 45th wedding anniversary. It consisted of a young just married couple from Belgium; Sadie and me; and a gal, Margaret, from Germany who was celebrating her 25th wedding anniversary without her husband because he had to stay home and take care of his public relations business.

Margaret spoke English very well. Margaret and Sadie and I became very good friends. We had an affinity. She had a good sense of humor. The situation was interesting because she was German and we were Jewish. We were honest with each other. It was 1973 and the war was over in 1945. The Nazi thing hangs over the air anyway. It was intriguing because in spite of that, we discovered a liking for each other. She was very friendly to us. The feeling was that she wanted somehow to make amends for the treatment of the Jews in Germany. I find it's harder to carry the burden of hatred than not. I didn't create the situation. We were touring in a car together. We were assigned to a guide who had a car that could accommodate six people.

The connection between Jews and Germans is a lot stronger than we realize because the Yiddish language is a derivative of the German language. The Jews of Europe are classified as Ashkenazi. Ashkenazi in Hebrew means "German". She and her husband Fred visited us in

Beverly Hills three times. He was a very nice man. She had a much stronger personality but he was very nice. When we visited them in Germany, about three or four times, he paid for everything. One time we spent time at their vacation home which was a village where they had a farm house. By the same token, when they were here, we hosted them. We spent some time at our condominium in Palm Springs. I got a nice letter from her once or twice a year besides a Christmas card. When Fred died she called us. When Margaret died, her sister called, saying she had been given special instructions by Margaret to call us. Of course I had called her at Sadie's passing.

We celebrated our 50th anniversary at the Biltmore Hotel, where we had our honeymoon after our religious marriage. We invited a lot of people. We had dinner, with a band and dancing. Some Italian friends came from Chicago whom we had met on a trip to India, the Stefanis. He was a doctor. She and Sadie both loved jewelry and they became very close friends. They did everything that was Jewish for us and we did everything Christian for them, in terms of cards and such. For our anniversary party, they stayed here with us and went to the party with us in a limousine. Our three kids put on that party and they got the limo. I wouldn't have. I don't feel comfortable drinking more than two or three drinks, so driving is not a problem. I got drunk one time in my life and I didn't like it. Sadie and Doreen talked quite often by phone. Every five years we did something big for our anniversary.

Sadie in Mexico, 1981

For our 60th we rented an exclusive ship out of Marina del Rey that catered to anniversary celebrations. We cruised around Santa Monica Bay, with only our party. There was a galley on the boat and they cooked up a dinner while we were on board. There was a band, and a dance floor. It was built as a party boat, with no sleeping facilities. We got out there about six or six thirty and came home close to eleven. We invited about eighty people. We had a one hundred-person boat.

1984

Our 65th anniversary we celebrated at the Friars Club in Beverly Hills. It was private club consisting of actors and comedians mostly. The members could go and have dinner there and in the process you met other members. It was a men's club but the members invited their wives and families. The Friars Club had a good reputation of catering affairs. They did a grand job for us. We had dinner and a professional, well known band with dancing.

For our 70th we went back to the Biltmore for a quieter affair with the kids, their families and our helpers. We had a private room to accommodate ten people. They had different sized rooms to accommodate different occasions. The food is good there. The Biltmore was aware that we were celebrating our 70th anniversary and our honeymoon there 70 years before. We received a very nice book made just for us. They treated us very nicely. There was a nice letter from the president or manager or whoever he was, thanking us for visiting 70 years later.

Our last anniversary was the 72nd which we celebrated at home with the family. We had Greek food brought in. Sadie was alert as always. That was one of the things that bothered me; she had to be suffering of boredom if nothing else. She listened to a lot of music. She was a very nice woman, always friendly. She had

her limit but it took a long time for her to reach it. Sadie was never two-faced. For example, she could not tolerate bigotry. She would put up with a lot before she gave up on somebody.

Sadie had a stroke in 1990 and did well for the first six years. After that we got caregivers. We traveled anyway. We took eight different cruises in five years with our caregiver, Aleli, with us. On the last cruise Sadie lost her sight. I never wanted her to die, yet her quality of life was poor. Death was a release; freedom.

Sadie and I used to share a "Klondike" ice cream together. We would eat it together at the same time so that between the two of us, our lick s would keep ahead of the melting ice cream. After Sadie died, I lost some of my Klondike ice cream to melting.

Chapter 12: Selling Subscriptions

My boss and friend, Jack Perlman, wanted me to go to San Francisco with him to work in the newspaper business, to give our territory a rest. We would sell the Call Bulletin, a Hearst Paper. I went up in the summer of '33, with the crew. Sadie went to live with her mother because there was no point her having an apartment and paying $25 a month, a lot of money. There is a bundle of letters that I sent to Sadie while I was in San Francisco which she saved.

I was in San Francisco for two segments: in 1933 and 1934; once with Jack Perlman and once with Ben Sharp; more than a year with Ben. There were two kinds of crews: local and traveling. Jack was more of a local crew leader. You went home every night. With Ben we worked territories. We stayed in a hotel.

In Los Angeles we would go out twice a day, once in the morning and once in the afternoon. There were about six in the crew. Jack would use a big car to take us to the territory. We drove up to San Francisco in his car.

Some guys who had been with Jack for years would work their own territory but reported to him. Jack's office was at 11th and Broadway. The kids just out of high school would get there somehow

Ben Sharp and Crew on Vacation

(thumbing a ride) and go with Jack to the local territory. The best time to work was between 4:00 and 9:00 p.m. Everyone was home then and seemed to be most sympathetic. We would work the business area in the morning, from about 10:00 a.m. to 1:00 p.m.

Ben's territories in the San Francisco area were fresh territories; different cities. I didn't repeat the same area. If you went to the same territory even a year later they would remember you and make some remark. It could be embarrassing. Once in a while they knew what you were up to, especially college kids, because they used to do it themselves! College grads used to sell magazines with similar stories because they were trying to get through school.

After two months in San Francisco everyone wanted to go home to see their relatives. I worked with Jack for a while in Los Angeles and then, after talking it over with Sadie, I decided to go back to San Francisco. I was doing pretty well in San Francisco when Jack and his crew decided to go home. Some of the other guys also liked it better in San Francisco.

San Francisco was sort of a "labor-minded" area. No matter what you did for a living, you were part of "labor." The people responded better than the L.A. people did. The Depression was on. There was more of a liberal attitude. In L.A. they had to spend $1.25 for the paper. In San Francisco, they had to pay less than a dollar; 75 cents.

Working for Jack – Good stories sell subscriptions

I worked on Jack's crew, either selling subscriptions to Hearst's Examiner newspaper, or collecting subscription money owed. He thought that since I was married, I would have to stick around because I would have to make a living.

I made up a logical story as a selling pitch and most people bought it. It was in the middle of the Depression. Jobs were not only scarce, they were non-existent. This job was available because it didn't cost Hearst anything. The company didn't pay me a salary; they paid me a commission. For collection of subscription money I would get a fee. If I sold a subscription, I would get a dollar and sixty-five cents. So it behooved me to sell subscriptions.

The Examiner cost a dollar and a quarter a month. I had to sell the customers on the idea of investing a dollar and a quarter for one month in order to get the commission which was a dollar sixty-five! There is a government agency called the "ABC" which stands for Audit

Bureau of Circulation. Every newspaper had to report, truthfully, how many paid subscribers there were to each paper. What the paper could charge for advertising was based on circulation figures. The larger the base, the more people would read the ad. The newspaper business made more money out of the ads than the $1.25 for the subscription or my $1.65 commission because the newspaper is full of ads. The company had to maintain the ABC figures to get the money from the ads so that's why they had us selling subscriptions.

People wouldn't buy a subscription without a story. Under Depression circumstances you couldn't say, "I'm soliciting for newspapers and I'd like you to take the newspaper for one month. It's only a dollar and a quarter." They would look at me like I was crazy. "I don't want a newspaper. If I wanted to buy one I would have had one!" You had to appeal to their good nature, to their willingness to help me out; it had to be a personal thing.

Jack organized the crew and he would take us out to a territory where we would hit the streets selling subscriptions. We each had our own little story. Generally you went with somebody else when you first started out, somebody who was a good producer, who had a good story. Then you would create your own story, not wanting the same story.

My story was that I wanted to get a job delivering papers but that I had to have a bond. Since I didn't have the money for a bond I was given the opportunity to sell ten subscriptions in lieu of the bond. The subscription only had to be for one month. If they ordered the paper for one month I would get credit for it. I had sold six and only needed four more!

Some of the stories were atrocious! For example, a story of one of the most productive guys was that his father had just died and was lying on the kitchen table. The guy needed money to bury his father! This kid could cry on demand. He was a great actor. Not everyone could tell that story without laughing!

Unions were starting to be very strong. Now they're not as strong because the government took over most of their stuff. For example, the union insisted that you pay time and a half for overtime. The law now is that you have to do that, so you don't need a union to get paid time and a half. Little by little the law took a lot of the union stuff over.

I got a car, a Packard. I thought maybe I could start my own sales group. The way Jack and Ben made money is that they had an override. They were called recruiters. For every order I wrote, I got a dollar and sixty cents. The recruiter got fifty cents on every one I wrote. If they had ten guys, and the ten guys wrote twenty orders, recruiter got $10. The other ten guys got maybe two dollars.

I decided to try my own luck as a recruiter. However, when I got there, I couldn't. Who do you go to? Everybody who did that kind of work was already working, either for Ben or for somebody else. I had to work myself and didn't have time to get anybody else. I couldn't get a crew. I drove back to L.A., got rid of the Packard and went back to San Francisco on the bus, to work for Ben. The effort to be on my own just fizzled out.

With Ben, who was a nice guy and all that, you had more opportunity than working for Jack in L.A. because you had a broader reach and could go to different territories on a regular basis.

In July of '34 there was a well-known strike in San

One Drunk Weekend in S.F.

One time on a weekend in San Francisco, a guy brought a big jug of Muscatel, a sweet white wine, to our card game. Up until that weekend, I had never really done much drinking to any extent – I didn't even know what a cocktail was. And if I did have a drink, it was 'Russian style', where you took a jigger of something, like scotch or vodka, took a swig, and that was it. Vodka was a Russian drink. For example, if it was cold out, or it was rainy, or something like that, you'd take a shot so that your body would get warmed up. I didn't keep tabs on drinking; it never made a big impression on me.

So this guy brought this wine and we were playing cards and drinking, and without realizing it, I got drunk. And the odd thing about Muscatel is that if you drink water the next day, you get drunk all over again. So it wound up being a very long weekend, like the "lost weekend." Friday night we drank, Saturday night we were hung over and drank water, and then it started all over again! It was the first time I ever got drunk — without really meaning to! I don't even really remember whether I had fun or not.

Francisco which involved all of labor. It involved the stevedores. Everything was closed down. There was nothing to do. So we decided to go on vacation. That's when we had the party, with Ben. We had been working in Petaluma and had a good run. We had done well and we all felt good. We had a nice dinner and went back to the hotel and went to somebody's room. It might have been Ben's room because he was the center of things. Somehow or other we started a water fight; someone threw a glass of water at someone and the other guy threw it back at him...before you knew it everyone was all wet and laughing. Ben, a big guy who was like a kid although he was 20 years older than we, was in the thick of it.

Apparently someone who had heard all the laughing and screaming, complained and the manager came up to see what was going on. When the manager saw what was going on he asked us to leave and we ultimately did because everything was so soaking wet we couldn't sleep there anyway! The hotel manager asked Ben to pay $100 for damages. Ben tried to fine us for starting it, each giving up $10 but we said, "No Way!" So Ben paid. He was paying the bill anyway. We moved out of there that evening. That was a lot of fun and I'll never forget it!

I went right away with Ben to different cities all over Northern California. After about a year, when I was already entrenched with him, when the occasion came up to give me a special situation, I always got it because I had been with him a long time and I was married. He did what he could to help me make a little more money than anybody else.

One time I went to Sacramento regarding the Call Bulletin, the daily afternoon newspaper from Hearst in San Francisco. It was a pretty good seller in Sacramento because Hearst would put the first two or three batches on a plane and deliver it to Sacramento each day an hour off the press where the Sacramento newspaper businesses would pick it up at the airport.

I was the only one on the plane with the pilot. I was going to collect some subscription money owed and in the process, making friends and all, I would also get them to renew their subscription. I would tell them, "I wasn't there to put them in jail or anything, just that the company would like their money!" The ones that paid said, "Oh, I'm sorry," and paid it, so it was still a friendly situation. I wasn't threatening them. So then I would say, "Well, how 'bout renewing for another month? You're probably used to it," or something like that. So it was on a friendly basis, to get them to renew. Not everybody did. In some cases, I wouldn't even ask them. If they were bad payers, they wouldn't pay me either. If I decided if they made a fuss about having to pay me, I never asked them to renew. Why waste your time?

Ben operated out of San Francisco with a crew. Wherever we went, we had three cars. We drove together to all other places and were gone from Monday to Friday. If you had been with him for a while and he had confidence in you, he would let you go on your own. The Sacramento trip, flying by myself, was a special treat. You could make arrangements with the pilot, the Call Bulletin plane pilot to meet you at the airport at a certain time. Ben would take me to the airport and pick me up when I got back.

I didn't consider the work I was doing hard, but you weren't sitting around. You were either lucky when you got orders and that was great or you weren't and you were down in the mouth. I might consider shoveling all day long working on a road hard work, but this was not like that.

Being a newspaper solicitor for Hearst was not a career I was looking for and Sadie's family didn't like what I was doing. But it was the only thing that was available to do during the Depression. Bitsy, Sadie's sister, read in the paper that they were giving exams for a Post Office position, which they hadn't done for years. Bitsy didn't like that her brother-in-law was working as a solicitor. It didn't look good for her. In any case, I really didn't like being a solicitor for Hearst. It was a dishonest sales pitch. I didn't harm anyone and I didn't steal anything and the customer got something for their money, so I didn't feel it was really a fraud. I didn't feel that my story was that bad (compared to the father lying dead on the kitchen table!) yet it still elicited some sympathy.

Bitsy suggested that I try for a Post Office position, so I came back to L.A. to take the exam. It was towards the end of 1934. She may have called me about it in January advising me that there would be a test the following May. So I didn't have to rush back to L.A. I had plenty of time. I worked in San Francisco and when the time came, went down and took the test. There was one doubt. You had to pass certain physical tests, one of which was you couldn't be colorblind, and I'm colorblind. That was not in the first test because they didn't care until you were a permanent employee. I took a literacy test to get in, but not a health test. They don't want you in there if you can't read. In order to work the Post Office you had to be literate.

They ask you questions about history or government or who's the president – whatever, even terminology, for example, "What is an address?" The ones who pass the test go on a list. Then, every time they need some workers, they go to the list. They pick them from the top down, according to how the applicants scored on the test. So, in April of 1936, I got called. I was proud because I was fourteenth on the list, out of maybe 200 or something. I got called much sooner than a lot of the others.

Meanwhile, I quit the job in S.F. and went to work for my father in L.A. I wanted to be in L.A. if the Post Office called me. The test wasn't that hard. Lots of people applied. I got a good grade. Right after San Francisco we lived with my parents again for a short time. I got a salary working for my parents, based on my need. I was only paid about 12 dollars a week or so. I could afford to be on my own and I was. I could rent a place. That's when Sadie got pregnant.

Chapter 13: Back in L.A.

We were in San Francisco until 1935. It was in 1935 that my folks bought their store on 4th Street. Sadie and I moved to Dittman Street, renting a little one-bedroom house in the back of another house. I had about $100 in the bank. Sadie got pregnant with Marvin there in '35 and he was born in '36. I worked at the store, which gave my father a chance to go out and buy more chickens. I don't know if my parents "made room for me" at the store or not. They did not pay me very much, but it was enough to get by. I worked there while waiting for a call from the Post Office. I had been making good money working as a solicitor compared to what other people were making. Now I really took a cut!

It was a hard time. In April of '36, after two months, I was called to work for the Post Office but was only guaranteed two hours a day. It didn't take very long for me to advance at the Post Office and enable us to go on our own. The basis of getting along on what you could afford was not getting sick. You didn't go to the doctor. If you got a cold, you took care of it yourself.

My dad helped me with what I needed. For example Sadie went to the doctor during her pregnancy. That was anticipated and taken care of. I had transportation. I didn't have a problem except that my income was rather limited. At Hearst if you wanted to get more money you just worked a little harder.

My parents let me go when I got the job at the Post Office and we couldn't afford the rent on Dittman. I helped my Dad out on Tuesdays, going to get chickens. It was more filial duty than anything at this point. Dad gave me chickens and eggs to take home, which amounted to a luxury at the time. Chicken was a cut above hamburger.

Post Office jobs had three classifications: a regular, a sub and a temporary. The Post Office in 1936 was no different from anywhere else as far as the Depression was concerned. They only guaranteed two hours a day...if you were called. They called me about five days a week. I had been working at the Post Office for about two months. The job wasn't very good because there wasn't much work. If they called you, they had to pay you for two hours. Sometimes they didn't call you.

There was no money. It was zilch. It was bad. It was the only time I felt the Depression really get to me because of the money. We went to live with Sadie's parents. The only money I got was the money from the Post Office. The savings I had from San Francisco was used up for Marvin's birth. Those two or three months when I was working as a temp were rough. This was the hardest time of my life, money-wise. It was hard for everybody.

We lived with Sadie's folks in West L.A. while she was pregnant, maybe three or four months. Bitsy and Mae also lived there but not Nellie; she was already married. Sadie's father was still okay in business. The new season was coming out and he came out with this new design and it went over but nobody bought. The kids were helping. Mae was working. Bitzy was working. Jerry was in a private business college to learn how to be a public accountant. Chuck, Mae's boyfriend, was working for his brother in San Diego at a shoe store. He came home on weekends to be with Mae. So Chuck lived there too, over the weekend. It was a very nice place, big, with three or four bedrooms. When Chuck and Mae got married, they got their own apartment, around the corner. Chuck was about five years older than Jerry. Chuck became a public accountant also. Nobody became a Certified Public Accountant at that time because they couldn't afford more schooling.

I worked very hard at the Post Office and did well. I didn't fool around and they gave me more work, more than the two hours a day guaranteed. The supervisor saw that I was a hard worker and gave me the opportunity to work the graveyard shift for eight hours, full time.

The Post Office paid better than anybody else at the time. After a year or so went by, I became a substitute instead of a temporary. Now I was a permanent employee and had to pass the health test, which I passed okay except for the color determination. I called a purple stamp blue. However, they gave me a second chance because I had already made my mark in the Post Office. I was already working the graveyard shift and they didn't want to lose me. They had a list of people they wanted to retain regardless of whether they were colorblind or not.

When I became a regular, I got $2,100 a year, which was about $.72 an hour. When I worked at the deli, at $2.00 a day, I was getting $.25 an hour.

Because I was working the graveyard shift I got home at five or six in the morning. I didn't get up until about one in the afternoon. Nobody was there; they were working. When they were there, after dinner, I went to work. So I wasn't in the family because of my hours and was not privy to the business problems of Sadie's father, who died in '42.

After Sadie had Marvin in July of 1936, we stayed with her family only about 6 or 7 days longer. Then we got an apartment down the street from Sadie's mother, on Edgewood Rd. We were there three or four months. It was a one-bedroom apartment, bigger than we had had before. We shared the bedroom with the baby, Marvin. Then we found this place on Westhaven.

By then I had made progress. I was always a good worker. I tried to do as much as possible so that not only did I get satisfaction out of doing good work but it attracted attention. My bosses spotted that right away and knew they could rely on me. It was not my goal to "get around" the job and get paid for doing nothing. There were a lot of people like that.

Even though I was a sub, I got a full-time run on the graveyard shift, which was not a popular shift. At the Post Office jobs went up for bid and went by seniority. None of the regulars bid on the graveyard, so they gave it to someone with less or no seniority such as myself. My boss said, "If you want to work on the graveyard, we'll put you on for eight hours." How could I turn that down? I went to work at 5:00 in the evening, when the mail came in. I started out at what was called the Arcade Annex, the working Post Office for Los Angeles. There were three shifts and I worked graveyard. When the mail came in it had to be cancelled. From upstairs the guys dumped the mail down a chute from the mail bags onto the middle of what they called the facing table. Everyone grabbed the mail, creating space for more letters to come down the chute. We stood around the table and

With the Family, 1945

put the letters face up into a slot under the table so that the stamp was in the corner and the slot was on a belt that went around and around and the mail accumulated at the canceling machine where someone would put it in the machine to cancel the stamp. From the canceling machine the mail was picked up to go through another sorting. Working at the facing table was an entry position at the Post Office because you didn't need any knowledge.

During that time Manny got involved with the chicken business. He was still in high school. At times one of us would stay at the shop and one of us would go with Dad to get chickens.

While I was on the graveyard shift at the Post Office, in late 1939, one of Dad's connections, from whom Dad used to buy turkeys, wanted to sell out. He wanted to sell every turkey on the ranch. He gave Dad a good deal, selling him a couple of thousand turkeys, right around Thanksgiving. I think the price he paid was by the turkey, for example, $1.00 a bird. He might have bought about a thousand turkeys for a thousand dollars. Dad was able to fill his store with turkeys and also the backyard. It was a big backyard. He made a good deal of money with this transaction. By keeping them and feeding them they regained the weight they had lost en route. This had to be a great number of turkeys because it was a big deal and he made a lot of money. Dad made an agreement to pick up the turkeys little by little. Manny was involved in the "turkey deal." That came along out of the blue and made all the difference in the world. It was a once-in-a-lifetime situation because the guy practically gave the turkeys away. Dad not only sold the turkeys to everybody that wanted them but he sold them wholesale to the big markets that did the dressing.

About then refrigeration came along. (At first it was ice.) Up until then you had to buy live chickens because there was no refrigeration. You had to buy fresh-killed whether you went to a kosher or non-kosher store. Manny was still at home helping my father. He was the helper instead of me. He went to the country with him; found the guy who had the chickens; made a deal and away they went. I was working at the Post Office.

Not much later he closed up the store and bought a four-flat on Gardner Street off Beverly Blvd. From there on in he was semi-retired. I used to go with him twice a week to get chickens. Manny was already going to college so he wasn't there to help him. He just picked a few of his best customers and served them. Since I worked nights at the Post Office, I could go with him. I did that for a long time. I worked at the Post Office on Saturday so I could help him out on Tuesday. That's when he went; for that I got a chicken and eggs. I don't remember him paying me anything.

Pa was in the chicken business for a long time. It was a long drive to Hemet for the chickens, a full day's work, although little by little he would get closer into Riverside. He finally gave it up in the early '50's. They were living in the four flat, collecting rents from the other three apartments. That's why he could afford to work just two days a week.

Later he bought an eight or ten flat on Detroit and 6th Streets, one block west of La Brea.

My parents were active in the "Workman's Circle" from the time of New Brunswick. They were liberal all their lives, socializing with people with the same point of view in the Workman's Circle. The Workman's Circle was a Jewish organization based on the Jewish traditional value of work. They had bazaars for charity and they patronized a resort in Ontario called Paradise Inn where my parents vacationed. The Workman's Circle had an agreement with Paradise Inn whereby they would give them business as a group and get a discount. The Paradise Inn benefited from the business and the Jewish organization didn't have to worry about discrimination.

Workman's Circle

When I first started to work at the Post Office I worked in the Arcade Annex on Third and Central. During that time they were building a new Post Office downtown at Macy and Alameda called the Terminal Annex. When that was ready everybody moved there. I was working downtown until 1939, when I had a chance to move to a station and work day shifts.

I bought a new Plymouth in '40, the last year they made automobiles until the end of the war. I think it was a tan color. The automobile factories became munitions factories.

At Christmas time Sadie used to work at the Post Office delivering packages (I got her the job) and once while she was delivering a tree fell on our car! Our new Plymouth! Our insurance paid to fix it. I never thought of asking the Post Office to pay to fix the car. That was during the War, around 1944. I was working at Station "D" which is now called Dockweiler. At that time it was at Jefferson and Vermont. I started working there in '39 and in '41 the United

Victory Garden

When I was working at the Post Office and living on Dunsmuir, the war had just started and everybody was putting in what they called "Victory Gardens." My daughter Barbara was about two years old. The house was a pretty nice house with a driveway on the south side of it and a garage in the back. Along the side of the house we had poinsettias, the long sticks with the flowers on top. They're very pretty but they're prolific and as a consequence they got heavy and were bending over the driveway so when you were driving they would scratch the car. I had decided to take them out. What should I do with them? They're long sticks, maybe ten feet tall. So I put them behind the garage.

About two years later, when these branches were dried out sticks, I decided to put in a Victory Garden, so I dug up the back yard and I put in some string beans and I thought, I'll put these sticks in to support the green bean vines. It took a long time for the beans to come up but I started getting poinsettias. Dried out pieces of wood came to life before the beans.

There was also an old dried up peach tree in the middle of my Victory Garden which I had to work around. I watered the garden and the peach tree got plenty of water along with the garden just like the poinsettias. That season Sadie, the kids and I had one big beautiful peach. A lot of stuff came up in that garden. Corn came up nicely, and eggplant, and lots of tomatoes which had to be cleared of tomato worms, which can be pretty big. Ultimately, we even got the string beans. So many soldiers were at war that there was a limited labor market. By growing things to eat and feeding yourself, you saved food for the soldiers. It was a patriotic thing to do and if you had more than enough for yourself, you could feed others who couldn't have a Victory Garden.

States joined the war. During those two years I always worked hard. The Post Office had supervisors over supervisors. The head supervisor from the Postmaster's office, whose name was Al Maynard, really liked me. He watched me work; he saw how I worked; he saw my relationship with the carriers and everybody else. He had a lot of confidence in me. Al Maynard would check on different Post Offices and see how the supervisors handled everybody.

When the war broke out about 6 or 7 fellows left to go to war, just out of station D. I became the key man in that Post Office. By then I already had two children. Even so, I felt that I could get to be an officer by making an application to the Officer's Training Corps. One of the guys did that and he became a lieutenant and he was assigned to the APO, which is the Army Post Office. So I applied, putting down all the information regarding where I worked, who my employers were, etc. Anyway, Al Maynard comes over and says, "What's this about you joining the army?" I said, "Well, you know." He says, "We're not going to let you go. We need men here too." Meanwhile the clerks in my office who had left were replaced by women who didn't even take the Civil Service Test. They were just hired off the street because they needed people.

Al says, "Who do you think is going to teach these women what to do? We gotta have somebody in here that knows what's going on." There was one supervisor who was an old man and he couldn't do everything. We had about forty carriers and we had about four service windows open all the time. And then there was the back help. There were a lot of people in there who needed supervising and the Post Office wouldn't let me go. It was a government agency and they had to release me in order for me to get into the Army and they wouldn't release me. In a manner of speaking I was drafted into the Post Office.

From our residence on Edgewood, we moved to a duplex on Westhaven. Barbara was born on Westhaven, in 1940, a year before the war. From Westhaven we moved to Dunsmuir, right around the corner, half a block away, but it was a nicer place. Then we bought Westhaven a year later. We sold Westhaven about '46 or '47 and moved into an apartment on 6th Street that my father owned. We lived there a couple of years until 1949. In 1949 I was promoted to supervisor at the Post Office. When my father gave me back the money I had loaned him after selling the Westhaven place, I bought the place on Bellingham, North Hollywood, where we lived from 1949 until 1954.

When I started working at the Post Office I let Sadie "run the store" at home. I gave her my checkbook and I just wanted five dollars for my pocket money. About a year later she gave me back the checkbook and said, "You run the show." She couldn't make it the way she was spending the money. So I started getting money from other sources. I started building poker tables on the weekend and would sell them to and through friends. They weren't cheap from

Terminal Annex, 2009

the store. I didn't want to spend the money to buy one so I made one. People liked it and I could make them to sell because I had no overhead. I bought whatever tools I needed to do the job. I needed a special kind of screw driver. It became a simple operation after a while because I had the materials, like long strips of aluminum and the wood. After that I started making cornices for drapes with sheets of plywood. You put the batting on and staple the cloth on. Someone asked me if I could do it. I figured if somebody else could do it, I could do it. For example, I cut scallops with a jig saw out of wood. That lasted quite a while. Every time I hung them up somebody saw them and wanted to know who did it and so they would tell them and the next thing I know I had another customer. I needed to make a little extra money here and there. These customers were one-shot deals.

When we were on Westhaven, it was a small duplex and there were a lot of things I could do to fix it up. For example there was an electrical outlet for a washing machine or whatever on the porch. We had one of those round washing machines. We didn't have an outlet in the bedroom. I knew enough about electricity to know that I could use the outlet on the porch. All I had to do was connect to it and I could have an outlet in the bedroom. So I made a little hole there, connected the wires and I put an outlet in the bedroom for a bed lamp.

In the kitchen, the stove was up against the wall and the wall was always a little bit splattered which you can't help, especially if you fry something. So I got some oilcloth that had the design of blue tile squares. I bought a sheet of it and put it behind the stove with metal strips so it looked like it had tile.

I figured finding out how to do things was better than trying to figure it out on your own because there are better and easier ways to do it; I went to school to find out. I went to one term, two nights a week, at Metropolitan High learning about carpentry. It was downtown on Washington Street. I learned about lumber and how to handle it. This was about '38 or '39. My project was to make a bread board. You have to put borders on it to stabilize it and keep it from buckling, then smooth it out. I built a house trailer for us, a fourteen-footer. In the summertime, when I was off Saturday and Sunday (it was a rotating thing at the time) we'd go up Friday afternoon to Carpentaria.

Later I was promoted to be Assistant Superintendent. Before I had been third man, now I was second man. The money increased. I left Station "D" because Al Maynard wanted to push me up. He liked me because I was a good worker. I didn't fool around and whatever I was told to do I did it. I understood what they wanted me to do. A lot of times you tell someone something to do and he misreads you.

He got me a job at the main office. My job was at the Postal Savings window. At that time you could open a savings account at the Post Office and you got a certain amount of interest. It was not the most popular program because not that many people knew about it and you had to go downtown to the Post Office whereas banks were available elsewhere. My job was to take deposits, let people make withdrawals and open accounts. This was a job away from the hum drum and I had to learn something new.

I didn't like this job at the window at all. It was the most boring job I ever had. I had to stay in the cage. Maybe one guy would show up during an hour, maybe 8 for the whole day. I started getting migraine headaches from boredom. I would help people from other windows with their work. There were money orders to be counted. I learned how to count them by spreading the cards out on the table. There was a table we worked at away behind the windows. If somebody came to my window, I got up and took care of them. The money order clerk happened to be a girl. When somebody came to her window, she would wait on them. We worked together when neither one of us was busy.

However, I was under the eye of the Postmaster at the Main Office. People got to know me. Al wanted me around there so that when things happened, he could do something. He really liked me. I liked him too. He was a wonderful guy. Al was the age of my father, maybe older. He died about a week after he retired, at 65. He was Irish and had a son who came to work for me too.

I told Al I wasn't very happy with it and he says, "Well, hold on a while." He gave me work from some of the other windows to keep me busy. Meanwhile, somebody retired from the Building Superintendent's Office at the Terminal Annex. The executive offices were at the Main Office in a high rise building on Main Street and the

Terminal Annex was the working Post Office, with 80 branches in Los Angeles. Now this was a much more interesting job. Al came to me and he said, "Would you like to work for Henry Meyer?" He was the Building Superintendent. Now that department had all the furniture, all the paper forms, and supplies. They had all kinds of forms. The whole basement of Terminal Annex was full of supplies and stuff like furniture and printing machines. The janitors worked from there. Al said, "If you want the job, you have to go to school for four months and learn how to draft." So I went to night school and learned drafting. With what I already knew and what I learned, I fit the bill. He felt that with my enthusiasm I would be good for this unordinary job. I got it without even bidding for it. This was a job on the road to promotion. When planning a new branch, you had to make a "footprint". In the footprint I had to design the floor plan for a new office. It was in the form of a "T". Most footprints are square. We had four windows: so much per window; and you had a mail drop. I drew the footprint for the "T" addition at Terminal Annex, a quarter inch to a foot, to scale. When they built a new Post Office, the toilets were already in, but the rest of it was not divided.

I was involved in this sort of thing because at Christmas time we had to dig out mail bags that we didn't need except at Christmas. We would also open up special offices then, neighborhood offices: we would rent a garage or whatever. The main office had places they used over and over. I had to arrange that new temporary facility long enough for a couple of clerks to operate. I used an established design. These stations only accepted mail. It went to Terminal Annex to be sorted.

At my new job I started changing things around. For example, I redid the whole sequence of forms by number. They liked that because anybody could get the forms they wanted by simply going by sequence.

Every day, superintendents would send in orders for what they needed and I would fill the orders. It was managing the Post Office supply warehouse as a clerk. Now that was a whole new world. As clerk to the Building Superintendent, everybody came to me for what they needed. For example, if a superintendent of a new station needed a desk, he would say, "Can you get me a new desk?" If I had a new desk, I would give it to him. So I got to know

Gertrude

Dave had been working in the Post Office before the War. During the War he went in the Navy and after the War he wanted to come to California, so he got transferred out here. We were friends for sixty years. David Berger's wife, Gertrude, was blind. She had become blind shortly after they were married, at age 22. They had two daughters and one got married and had a baby. Gertrude wanted to see the baby so she went to the doctor because she heard about some operation. He said, "Yes, I can operate, and yes, you can see, but not for more than a year. It will just go back to where it was. If you want to spend the money, and you want me to do it, I'll do it, but I want you to know it's not a cure; it's a temporary thing. She says, "Well, I don't care. I want to see my granddaughter. Go ahead."

So she had the operation and saw the baby and ultimately became blind again. We invited them over for dinner periodically. They came over in the meantime and she said, "The main reason we came over is because I wanted to see you. You've been a friend a long time and I don't know what you look like. She was very surprised and said, I had no idea you looked like that. Maybe it's your voice but I always thought of you as a chubby little man! More than that, she was surprised to see her husband because when she married him he was 22 years old and in the Navy. Now he was fifty. She couldn't believe how he had aged!

everyone in the Post Office and I made a lot of friends among the top echelon. Bill Green was the top supervisor from the Main Post Office. He was called the "Superintendent of Mails."

Bill Green also had an office at Terminal Annex. He did the promotions. It had to go through him or it didn't happen. We had ten thousand employees. He didn't know everybody. Next to him was the Postmaster. Bill Green called me on the phone where I was in the basement downstairs one day and said he needed two new desks. He was very impressed because I got the two best desks I could find and I had them delivered to his office within the hour. He wanted to know who I was. So I went to his office and talked to him, introducing myself to him. From then on in he knew who I was. I worked as a clerk to the Building Superintendent for about two or three years. I was in charge of all forms, all the paper needs, all the personal supplies and the furniture. It was a prestigious job. Out of all the clerks, there was only one job like that. It was from there that I was promoted as a supervisor to the special delivery at the Terminal Annex.

I knew not only how to furnish it and set up the forms, but I also knew about special delivery. By then I had established my reputation. Every time they had some sort of a promotional thing going I was involved in it.

For example, periodically the Post Office was checked over by the Postal Inspectors. They want to make sure that everybody follows the rules and that it's clean and it's this and it's that. So they included about twenty people, ten carriers and ten clericals. They teamed me with one of the carriers. Each clerk was teamed with a carrier, because now you had knowledge of both sides. It took about two months to check a group of stations. Even then L.A. had about 80 Post Office stations. We were given 8 or 10. We went in there and checked it out to make sure that everything was okay. We made a report on each one. We wanted to make sure that when the Postal Inspectors came they found everything okay.

They then moved me to the office at La Tierra on Crenshaw because it was new and I could establish the furniture and the closet with the forms. Before we opened up it was ready to go. There I was Assistant Superintendent. From there they moved me to Pico Heights.

There were a lot of smart people at the Post Office who used the Post Office as a bridge during the Depression. One became a well-known dentist and another became a famous patent lawyer. I had a friend, David Berger, who worked in the Postmaster's office. He knew the Postmaster very well. When he needed supplies for the Postmaster's office, he had to call me, so we became more acquainted. David interfaced with the supervisors. He used me to get attention from the supervisory people, which was okay because I got a benefit out of it too. He would say, "You need a desk? I'll get you a desk." He would call me and I would deliver it. Now they knew me as well as him.

At this time there was esprit de corps at the Post Office. There were clubs; maybe a fishing club or a bowling club, different things that people might be interested in. They created clubs that had dues. With the dues they would buy stuff for picnics. We were like a big family; all friends working at a job. It wasn't competitive, but friendly. In those days working at the Post Office was a community thing. We would have play days at the park. One time our play day was covered in the local newspaper and there I was, named most popular employee, which I don't remember, but there's the photo in Sadie's collection. From my office we operated different baseball team. My immediate boss was a social person. He was a very nice guy; he was an Assistant to Henry Meyers. Meyers was a political appointment. He did all the purchases. It was a big job. His office bought the desks. He would go to a furniture company and have them build the desks. My boss was sort of a social secretary for the Post Office. There are a lot of public relations involved. He had to maintain a level of camaraderie between all the superintendents. There were eighty superintendents. He kept peace. If there was any kind of a problem that Bill Green sensed, Charlie Stanbeck, the Assistant Building Superintendent, would go out and visit these guys; maybe take them to lunch, whatever, in order to maintain peace.

The difference between the old Post Office and the present Post Office is like the difference between a town and a big city. In a town, you knew everybody and everybody knew each other or at least something about each other. In a big city, you don't. That's exactly what's going on now.

The next opening that occurred for promotion to supervisor was in 1949 and I got it. My first assignment was as Supervisor to the Special Delivery section at the Terminal Annex. It was the only Special Delivery Section in L.A. at the time. I was in charge of the outgoing Special Delivery. Special Delivery mail came to my department. Now it's called Overnight Delivery, or Express Mail. The job of Supervisor was a whole new line of work. I didn't like my first assignment that well because I was low man on the totem pole.

I had to cover whoever was off. There were five supervisors in the Special Delivery section. The top supervisor was Bartholomew. He worked days. He had three assistant supervisors. Whenever they were off, I would cover for them. It's a 24-hour job. I would work different times. Then, something happened. There were special delivery carriers who used their own cars to deliver. I noticed there was something wrong in the amount of letters they were able to deliver. One guy would get a batch and be back in two hours and wanted more. Another guy would take a small batch and be back in two or maybe three hours. During a meeting, I came up with the idea that maybe we should check them out. They said "OK, you go!" So I didn't have to come in day and night; I was assigned to go with the messengers and see why there was such variation in performance. I realized what was going on and made some recommendations.

For example, there was this one guy who was not a young man and he drove very erratically. After I went with him I came back and I said "This man can't do this job. He's going to get killed or something."

They had a number of walking routes out of downtown and I recommended that he be given one of these routes instead of way out in West L.A., driving. So they followed my recommendation and he was happier. He probably couldn't see very well. He was happy to get the metropolitan walking job. Again, it brought me into the spotlight.

Bill Green, the top man in the L.A. Post Office, gave me another position. At that time we finally got some money from the government for expansion. They started breaking down the stations. All the new apartments required more time for mail delivery, for example. Bill Green knew that I knew how to organize and that's why he promoted me to Assistant Superintendent for Rancho Park on West Pico. It was a brand new, big Post Office in a growing area and I had to set it up, as well as be in charge of the Special Delivery messenger service, which at a branch station was an experiment. They sent me there as a supervisor for two reasons. Number one, it was so far away from downtown that it had its own special delivery department so I was in charge of the special delivery. It was also one of the few stations that had three supervisors instead of two. There was the Superintendent and two Assistant Superintendents. So I was the second Assistant Superintendent. I was not an ordinary clerk anymore; I was in the managing department. I had to get along with everybody...or else!

I had to come in late. I would come in about 4:00 in the afternoon and close up about midnight. The place was closed after six. During that time I had a crew of special delivery messengers that came in to deliver the mail. When the truck came in around six to pick up all of the day's mail, he also brought special delivery mail from the Terminal Annex. When the messengers, about five men, came in about 7 or 8 o'clock, I gave them their last delivery. They delivered until midnight. I divided the mail into routes. There were about five deliveries per messenger. This was for the whole west end, La Cienega West. The lobby was open until midnight. In the lobby was a mail drop. The Post Office itself was a new design. They had modern, Swedish type furnishings, whereas the old one was oak. I put everything in order. I worked with the floor plan to see where to put things like forms. For example, I turned a closet into a supply closet. That had been my job at the Terminal Annex. So every time a new Post Office was established they sent me there to set it up.

The house on Bellingham, one block off Laurel Canyon, was brand new. It was the display house for the new block that had just been built. Eventually we added on a bedroom. My youngest son Bob was born there. It was an affordable area. The builder was living in it and he let it go for whatever it cost him. I went through the Hollywood Hills to work, about a half hour drive. My parents came to visit us every Saturday when we lived on Bellingham, my dad driving because my mother didn't drive. He had a new peach colored Plymouth. Once in a while Manny and Barbara would come with the kids.

From Rancho Park I went to the La Tierra station which is on Crenshaw and 54th. I was there a year or so and then they built a new station at Pico Heights and they

A Family Visit

sent me there. Los Angeles was expanding fast. For example, when I started, Station "E" was already 87 carriers. They split it into two and it became the Los Feliz Station and the Edendale Station. I moved around, always as the Assistant Superintendent at the new Post Offices, setting them up.

There were two types of night work. From 5:00 pm to 1:00 am was the heaviest load. We had several thousand people working sorting the mail at Terminal Annex. That was the heaviest work. The building was more than a block. All the mail from the city wound up at Terminal Annex and some from the County. That was when it went on the cancelling machines and to the first distribution and the second distribution.

Then there was the graveyard shift. You came in about 10:00 or 10:30 in the evening and worked until about 6:00 or 7:00 in the morning. This was different work. They worked the mail to the carrier. The first distribution was to go to different states. For example, they'd tie up mail for the state of Washington and send it off. Forget about the mail to all over the world, it's gone.

The L.A. stuff was broken down into the neighborhood Post Offices, stations. Whoever works the station has to know where the street goes. My section, working the graveyard shift at Terminal Annex was Station E from the beginning. My job was to break down the mail to the carriers. I got a bunch of mail that said "Station E". I took it to my desk and broke it down to each carrier.

They moved me to the Pico Heights Station for more than one reason. Bill Green was the superintendent of mails. He was the head man of the Post Office. The Postmaster was an appointee and he didn't know anything about the Post Office. Bill Green really ran the Post Office. He had a brother-in-law who was a mailman, a carrier. Bill Green pulled the strings in order to promote him to be the superintendent at the new Pico Heights station. There were three supervisors. He needed two assistant superintendents; one for the carriers and one for the clerks and the office. Bill Green gave me the job of Assistant Superintendent in charge of the clerks and the office. If there was a problem the clerks came to me. If there was a disgruntled customer, I would try to calm them down.

That meant that I was running the show because his brother-in-law had been a carrier and didn't really know how to run a Post Office. Bill Green knew that I knew how to do things so it cushioned his brother-in-law so that he could do no wrong, in a manner of speaking. I'm not trying to make myself a big shot but those are the facts. He didn't know anything, and I had to train him. One of the things I realized was that I would not get promoted any higher because Bill Green wanted to protect his brother-in-law.

The thing is, it made the whole office operate better if someone who knew what they were doing was in charge. As far as the Pico Heights Station, if it were ever checked by the Inspectors or anybody else, it would come out all right. I had the experience. Bill Green had confidence in me because I came through for him whenever he needed it. I was somebody dependable. This is one of the characteristics missing in a lot of people. They can be smart, they can be good supervisors but they're not dependable, for whatever reason. They would have to weigh something out and they would always weigh it in their own favor, rather than trying to solve the problem. As a manager, he didn't want to be bothered with the problem. Bill Green knew that I came through for him. The idea was to get his brother-in-law promoted and he chose me because he had confidence in me.

I noticed that there were a couple of promotions that went by and I wasn't even considered. This was around 1951 and I was starting to consider going into business for myself.

Chapter 14: Going Independent

In 1951, at the Pico Heights Station, I saw an opportunity to supplement my income, after having worked at the Post Office 15 years. I knew of two guys in the mail pickup and delivery business and they were doing real well. At that point, realizing that I wasn't going to be promoted, I decided to try it. I got mail delivery business on the side and I got Manny involved.

I knew what the guys in mail pickup business were doing because they would come and pick up the mail for their customers. They would ask for mail from their customers' boxes at the Post Office. I gave it some thought. I talked to Manny about it and he suggested we go ahead and try it and make a few extra bucks. I could solicit customers and he could make the deliveries.

Manny and I opened up business with three customers out of the Pico Heights Station in '51. We wanted to augment our incomes. Manny could make the deliveries in the morning before he went to work. Mail was available at 7 a.m. He didn't have to report to his office until 8 or 9.

I was at the Post Office, a supervisor already. We got settled with it very quickly and even got another guy whom we paid to pick up the nightly outgoing mail from the customers and bring it to the Post Office. This lasted maybe two months when the Postmaster found out about it because one of my competitors told him. Somebody wrote a letter and the Postmaster told Bill Green to take care of it. Bill Green told me it was a conflict of interest because I had an edge. I knew which businesses held Post Office boxes while the competitor had to find out who they were. The Post Office had rules.

I had to make a choice: I either quit the Post Office and kept those three accounts or give up the three accounts which I had with Manny. In my wildest dreams I wasn't going to give up my job at the Post Office because I was already a supervisor. I was already making $5,200 a year. $100 a week at that time was a lot of money. I told Manny and he thought about trying it on his own but decided not to.

I stayed at the Post Office and worked a couple of more years. The concept of the mail delivery business stayed in the back of my mind however. It bothered me that it was a conflict of interest because it was not to my advantage. As the kids grew older I realized that there wasn't enough money for them to go to college. There just wasn't a lot of income to do anything. $100 a week was just a little bit better than breaking even because at least I could buy a car. While I worked at the Post Office I got time off during which I mostly did other things, like help my dad. It wasn't like I had a lot of vacation time.

Late in November, 1952, I wanted to investigate to see if it would be practical to go into the mail pickup and delivery business. In January of '53, I had two or three weeks of compensatory time. You didn't get paid for overtime; you got time off instead. For example, during the Christmas period, I would be working ten and twelve hours a day. But I wasn't paid any overtime as a supervisor. If I wasn't a supervisor, I would be paid overtime. As a supervisor, I got paid vacation.

I decided to conduct a

Focus

In 1949 TV's came in. We had friends, Ruth and Jerry Benjamin, who bought a television. When the Milton Berle show came on they made their living room into a kind of theater, and invited their friends to watch the show. We decided to get a television set but they were expensive so I got a kit and I started assembling it, using every spare moment. I was anxious to get it done so we could watch it. When I do something, I really focus on it. When I got home, I'd have dinner and get right to it. Sunday, I'd be on it all day long. I don't know why it took me so long. Each part has to be soldered and there are a lot of parts. Finally I had it finished. I had a TV for the kids. As a consequence of such strong focus, a lot gets by me that I'm not aware of. I'm sure Sadie wasn't too pleased with my intensity but she accepted it and felt it was worthwhile because of getting the reward.

survey to see if North Hollywood was practical, in the locale where I lived and not in competition with the Los Angeles business doing mail delivery. I went to businesses and said I was conducting a survey. The minute you say that you're not selling anything and you don't want money, you get an audience. I presented my business plan to them and asked if they would be interested in that kind of service. I asked about 50 businesses; everybody in North Hollywood that I could find. I promoted my service on the basis of my long experience with mail at the Post Office. I got three answers: "Yes, No, and Maybe." I found there was a very good possibility of a market. Then you called it a "survey." Now it's called "market research."

After I did the survey, I solicited in what you might call "virgin territory", territory that did not have a mail delivery service. I did the commercial as well as the industrial area. I opened up business with five or six customers in February of 1953. I started in North Hollywood and expanded from there. When there was no place else I could go in North Hollywood, I started in Burbank. Sadie ran the routes and I went to work selling.

When I started, I went to the customers who said "yes" and then went back to the people who said "maybe." I even went back to the people who said, "no," because now that I was in business, even the "no" people said "yes," if they felt there was a need for it. This service was no good to anybody that didn't need it. The thing is for them to evaluate the situation and decide whether they needed it or not. My objective was to do it cheaper than they can. That's the whole trick. I said I would do it for $15 a month which was a little more than 50 cents a delivery. They sat down and they figured, "Let's see, I pay the guy $5 an hour or even $4 an hour, whatever. I had a driver, paying him 75 cents an hour. So at that point, maybe they were paying him 75 cents an hour. If I were charging 50 cents, they would save 50%, so they decided, "Well, that's a good idea, I don't have to have a car, I don't have to pay insurance, I don't have to do anything." It was an offer they couldn't refuse.

Meanwhile, back in '46 my brother Manny married Barbara Wolfrom. Manny and Barbara got married in Las Vegas, en route to Chicago. In Chicago, Manny got his Master's degree in Social Service Administration. When he was there he got a job in New Orleans. He was gone for several years. He was a social worker in Los Angeles when he came back and sometime later he went to work for the Community Chest. When Manny came back the folks helped him buy the house in Sun Valley on Wixom Street. When Manny and Barbara lived in Sun Valley, I noticed that there was a "coolness" between us.

That's when I began to suspect that my mother was upset because I went into business without inviting Manny.

I had bought the duplex on Westhaven for five thousand in '43 and sold it for 11 thousand in '47. I moved into one of the apartments my folks owned on 6th street and Detroit, one block west of La Brea, while Pop borrowed my profits from Westhaven to buy the property he later sold to

Barbara, Manny, and our mother, 1946

Manny, which was an apartment building on Sherbourne that my folks moved into.

Pa paid me the money back after about two years when he sold the four-flat and I had been glad to help him. However, I was surprised that I wasn't consulted when they sold the Sherbourne property to Manny. I was annoyed because they never asked me about it, or told me about it. I just happened to find out. The fact that they kept quiet about it meant that they felt some guilt. After two years, in '49, when Pa paid me back, I bought the place on Bellingham.

My folks moved into one of the apartments on Sherbourne. It was a very nice neighborhood, almost Beverly Hills. It was early Los Angeles Spanish style. The grandchildren would visit them there and they would have Passover dinners there. Pa would sit in the kitchen and drink tea through a sugar cube in his lips, Russian style. He also liked to chew on the chicken bones, to get the marrow out. One time in the kitchen they opened up a box of black caviar sent from relatives in Russia.

My folks lived on Sherbourne until Pa died in 1962, about 14 years. We visited my folks there about once a week. After Pa died I visited my mother at her apartment on Hayworth.

My mother was upset with Sadie (instead of me) because she felt that we married too young. Ma was resentful. In the old country, marriages were arranged by the parents, as had been my parents' marriage. Sadie and I married when we did because it was a natural progression. We were in love. I was working and making a living. The Depression was a huge factor. Mother wasn't ready to let me go at eighteen years old, especially without consulting her. Eighteen years old is very young but it was the Depression. I think I was pretty much my mother's favorite until I married Sadie when Ma switched to Manny. There was a coolness between Manny and myself which then developed.

My mother was much more accepting of Manny's wife Barbara. She was the second daughter-in-law; by that time the damage had been done. Barbara was a college-educated girl, and pretty. Sadie was pretty too, but my mother accepted Barbara and not Sadie. In return Barbara accepted my mother and they became friends.

Chapter 15: A Disconnected Family

Sadie tried everything in the book to be friends with my mother. Sadie was a very friendly person. One time we were in Hong Kong and Sadie was walking down the street and this woman started talking to her. And so they talked! I was busy with something else; just the two of them were walking down the street and talking. I don't know why they exchanged names and phone numbers and addresses. Next thing you know, they're visiting L.A. She called up and Sadie invited them over.

However nothing worked with my mother. Superficially, she and Sadie were friends but my mother would egg me on to do something against Sadie's wishes. Later, in the '60's while we were living on Goodland, Sadie and I had our only argument. Sadie was very upset. My mother was always creating a situation where I had to make a decision in her favor or in Sadie's favor. I always made it in my mother's favor. This time Sadie was so upset she said, "You're either going to be my husband and live with me or we are going to get a divorce and you can go back and live with your mother!"

It was to that point. She was boiling mad and hysterical. I was taken aback because I wasn't expecting this. She started out by telling me that while I was at the office my mother and dad were visiting and that they had lunch together; they argued, and then they left. The issues never amounted to beans. It was just aggravation. For example, "My mother might say, "Pick me up at 3." Sadie would say "I can't pick you up at 3; I'll pick you up at 4." "No, if you can't pick me up at 3, pick me up at 5." That sort of thing.

When I got home for dinner that's when the argument started. Well, I'll never forget it because it made the difference in our marriage. Suddenly I had to decide whom I'm going to go with. I suddenly realized that my wife was more important to me than my mother. It was an attitude that my son Marvin caught on to because he became very, very protective of his wives, even when they were terrible and he knew they were terrible. He would still say, "Well, she's my wife."

I remember saying things to Sadie when we had the argument: "Why do I always side with my mother?" Sadie said, "Why do you always side with her?" I said "BUT SHE'S MY MOTHER!" The relationship is a blood relationship. You have to realize that that's an accident; whereas a marriage is not an accident. My mother was a pretty sharp woman. She always arranged for me to make the decision regarding who was more important. After all, my parents' relationship was not a "love affair marriage." Love comes later. It's like "Fiddler on the Roof," where, in an arranged marriage, all of a sudden he says "Do you love me?" She is surprised by the question "Do I love you?" After all, for twenty-five years I've been having your children, I've been baking your bread, I've been making your dinner, I've been cleaning your house! Do I love you? Would I do that if I didn't?" I don't know. That's the way it was. My parents seemed, as far as I could see, pretty compatible. The yelling seemed normal.

At that time there was a split between my mother and me. She thought, that's okay, I still have another son. She had felt abandoned by me when I got married. Her experience, however, taught her not to antagonize Manny's wife.

This split also caused a split between Manny and me. This is one of the saddest things of my life because there was no reason for it. The connection was still there...and the disconnection. That's the way life is.

Most relationships are strictly an accident. Some people you take to and some people you don't. Sometimes at business social affairs you made connections. Sometimes it was a contact that stuck with you for a long time, most of the time it was just "Hi, how are ya." It all depends, that's why I call it an accident. Sometimes a business connection becomes strictly a personal connection. It's necessary to have friends and business connections too. I had thousands of customers in my world, separate from the world I had with my wife. Sometimes they overlapped.

However, this coolness with Manny had begun long before. There was a four-year difference between us. This is a difficult difference because, for example, when you're fourteen and you start looking at girls and having pals, a brother of ten hasn't arrived there yet. I had to take care of him for many years and, to be truthful, I resented it. Generally, when young adults reach their twenties the gap narrows but that didn't happen with us because Manny went off in another direction from where I was. He was in college, I wasn't. The Depression affected it all.

This gap did however begin to close while Manny was still in Berkeley. On my vacation in 1940-41, I went to San Francisco and stayed at his place for a week. Manny had a girl friend, , who was much older. He took me around. Margo was a silversmith. She was very nice and once he took me to her house and he showed me her shop. Sometimes she would look under a microscope at, for example, water, to get ideas for her work from the microscopic images. Manny learned from her and he did a lot of jewelry making himself many years later. He even had a shop at home throughout his life.

I was working for the Post Office and Manny got his education and started working for the the Community Chest in Los Angeles. He started working for the Social

Margaret De Patta

"Margo" was Margaret De Patta, a seminal figure in the American Modernist Jewelry movement. She was a founding member of the San Francisco Metal Arts Guild and is widely acknowledged as a mentor to many of the Bay Area jewelers. Her architectural forms were influenced by the Constructivists. Her work is included in the collections of the Oakland Museum, The British Museum in London, The Museum of Fine Arts, Boston, The Renwick Gallery of the Smithsonian Museum of Art, and the Museum of Art and Design in New York.

Service where he met his wife Barbara. He had a job that consisted of helping young people "get home." Because of the Depression, kids ran away from home. They figured they could do better on their own, or at least now they wouldn't be a burden on their family. Not having any money, they used to hop trains, especially freighters. One of the things was that when they decided to get off the train and the train was moving, they would jump off the train. Very often, they would get hurt pretty badly. Manny was telling me once, he had this kid; they finally found out who his parents were and where they were. He was arranging to get the money to send him back home. The kid had a broken leg and he had a hell of a time trying to correct it. It was a bad case. I asked him, "Why did he jump off the train? Didn't he realize he could get hurt?" Manny said, "No, they don't. They watch movies, and in the movies people jump off the trains and roll around the ground and get up. They don't get hurt. The kids figure, if they can do it, I can do it. But they find out that the guy in the movie is using tricks."

Manny and Bernie 1936

Our interests were different. When I thought I would like to get into business for myself it was already 1952. I went into the Post Office in '36. Manny and I had been growing further apart. For example, while I was working at the Post Office. Manny married

Barbara and they went to Chicago where he got his Masters at the University of Chicago, and from there they went to New Orleans.

So we were apart for a good many years and there wasn't any correspondence. Once in a while there might have been a visit to the folks but they didn't necessarily share that with me. So from '36 to '53 is a long time, about 16 years. It was a long time before Manny finally wound up working here in L.A. and he had the time to work with me back in '51. At that time it was not only a temporary thing but I don't even know that we had a plan; it was really to make hay while the sun was shining. There was no official business deal or papers or anything else. It was just that we depended on each other without any papers because we were brothers. Between '51 and '53 when I opened up business in North Hollywood two years had gone by. Manny had a career going. We were in different social areas. We didn't have social contact. When he was in Chicago and New Orleans, we were far apart. When he came back, we didn't have much contact, because we had never had much social contact in our married lives.

When we were growing up it was like we were in different generations in a manner of speaking. Being four years apart, when I was sixteen, he was twelve. When I was twelve, he was eight. He wanted to hang on to me but to me as a kid, he was a pest. This is a common occurrence among all siblings. For example, when I was twenty and he was sixteen, he had a friend who influenced him to go from a "C" student to an "A" student. I had nothing to do with that. That was his generation that influenced him. The relationship between brothers ultimately comes together when you're both in your twenties, if you want it to.

It was many years later that I found out that Manny was angry with me for not asking him to join me in my business venture in 1953. I have a suspicion that my mother had influenced this feeling. She did nothing to bring us closer. Perhaps she said something like "You mean to tell me he didn't ask you to join him?" It could be that my father and mother resented that I didn't ask Manny to go into business with me because they wanted business to be a family affair. My father never worked for anybody else. The only time was for one year when he first came to this country, when he worked for the Michelin Tire Company because he didn't know what else he could possibly do. He saved every nickel so he could buy a horse and wagon and go into business on his own, no matter what, because he knew he would make it. My father believed that if you worked hard, and kept on going, and make friends and so forth and so on, you could make it.

Manny and I were both working with my father as we grew up. Manny would have liked to expand, but my father said no, let's just make a living, not capture the world. The basic philosophy was that we would be together: "Reznick and Sons." My parents never consulted or advised me. They never said, "You know what, you're going into business, why don't you ask Manny to join you?" Manny didn't think that way. He had a future in his own line of work. He was getting involved in bigger and bigger projects in fundraising, his expertise. He was already the head of the local Community Chest. He was going in a completely different direction.

When Manny and Barbara came to visit us the subject was never raised, so I had no idea that he was resentful. He never talked to me about it. He didn't tell me he was upset; we didn't have any discussion; I had no idea why he was all stand offish. It's obvious to me now that it was just plain old lack of communication.

My mother was resentful of Sadie; first of all because not only did we marry very young, but also without consulting our parents, or asking permission, which was against Jewish tradition, where marriages, such as my parents', were actually arranged by the parents.

My mother may have exhibited mischievous behavior in acting to create a chasm between her sons. The period of twenty years of not speaking to my brother and his family was touched off by their behavior when my wife Sadie became ill with skin cancer on her leg. I think, partly because of my mother's influence, and largely because of alienation, my brother and his wife did not call. His wife Barbara may have been involved also. I'm not sure there was any connection between our parents and her parents. There was always the specter of anti-Semitism. Not knowing people, one played it safe in assuming it existed. The relationship I had with Barbara was vague and distant. When Manny's kids came along, the holidays like Thanksgiving were celebrated with his wife Barbara's parents. There was very little social connection. When the family did come over it was more of an acquaintance, even a "duty" situation.

Sadie had a melanoma on her leg. Melanoma is a nasty form of cancer. It spreads very fast and was fatal ninety per cent of the time. Most skin cancers are not that big of a deal. Melanoma is. That's why they cut a large part out of Sadie's leg. After the operation she had to lie on her stomach for six weeks. She learned to suffer. Late in life she must have felt bad when she was unable to move, but I was afraid to ask her how she felt about her situation. What's the point of saying "How are you?" It's better just to say "Hi". That's about it. We had kissing. She couldn't do anything but listen to music. She could hardly hear anybody else, so her concentration was on music. She was responsive and very nice when you talked to her and she never complained.

Friends call. "How is she? Is everything all right?" I'm thinking to myself, "My own brother doesn't call. He doesn't care. He must know about it." I figured, "What's the point?" I don't call everybody and say "Sadie's sick" but people find out and they call me. It didn't have to be a social reconnect, but just a gesture, a symbol of caring, of belonging, of family relationships, of community. Even if he were still irate about my not asking him to join me in the business, which was years ago, this would have been a time to call. It was a matter of life and death. I didn't know what he was mad about or what the problem was. It may have been that they just didn't want to respond to anything unpleasant. I think that's true of most people. You have to care for someone to get involved if they're in trouble.

The split between our families lasted 20 years, until my mother's death. She never mentioned that there were bad feelings between Manny and me. She didn't want to know about it. She could have said something to me. It was all about hurt feelings on both sides. We were both at an age when we were building our future, with no contact between us.

My father wanted a close relationship with his sons. He would have loved any business that would have included his sons: "Aaron Reznick and Sons". However, during the Depression, it wasn't feasible. There wasn't enough business for more than one family. After Manny graduated, my father didn't want to expand the way Manny wanted. It didn't seem like a feasible dream to my father because his background was limited to a European village. He really didn't understand corporations. He didn't have a corporate mentality. Manny and I, on the other hand, grew up in the United States, in a democratic society where business flourished in many ways. My father wanted to be in control and he wanted to do business in a way he understood. When he was working in Russia, he had job security but no political security. We went our own ways.

When my mother was in her final home on Robertson, I would stop every day because it was on my way home. She was alone so I stopped. Manny was on the other side of town, sometimes working in Hawaii. So I became her main visitor.

Once she got sick, I dragged her around from one doctor to another because her original doctor simply said, "I can do nothing for her anymore, so don't bring her to me anymore." She had been going there every week. There was nothing more he could do. She was old. She had diabetes and she was sick. I was burdened with taking her to the doctor. It was always breaking up my day. I had a business to run. That was all right. She was my priority. Manny was far away in Palos Verdes, an hour from her. I was only about eight minutes away. I visited her about four or five times a week. I tried to make her have

118

some company, some discussion, something. Manny could have come down to see her but I'm not sure that he did.

So I got a hold of another doctor who took a fresh look. He examined her from scratch and told her she had a lung problem; she had fluid in her lungs. He told me to take her to his hospital, the Beverly Hills Hospital, and they got the fluid out of her lungs and she felt much better.

I came to see her the next day. She could breathe. She was feeling chipper and for the first time she said, "I appreciate your coming to see me." I said, "Well, I'm closer." I always left the office about 3:30, so I could stop by on my way home. "You're a good son," she said, for the first time in my life. She was sitting up in bed Indian style. The previous day had been difficult for her and also for me because I spent the whole day taking her from one doctor to another and finally winding up at the hospital.

It was a bewildering situation because I really didn't know what was going on. I didn't know what to expect. There wasn't time to be sad because I was involved in the situation. I was trying to save her. Manny was too far away. It was really just me and my mother.

That night her lungs filled up again. In the morning I got a call. They said she was very bad, to come. The doctor said that there was no point in going on with any more procedures. He wanted permission to unplug her life support. Sadie went with me and we had to make the decision. The doctor said she would not regain consciousness, so we unplugged. There really wasn't any choice. She didn't want those tubes in her. She was indicating that she wanted the oxygen tubes out. We left and she died about an hour later. The next time I saw her was at her funeral. I got a rabbi that was recommended to me. He turned out to be a very nice fellow. He asked Manny and me to tell him something about her because he didn't know her. I said she was resolute. She ran the show and she generally ran it in the right direction when we were kids. All her siblings looked up to her. She was really the leader of the pack. She was a regular strong woman. She was the head of the household but she made my father think he was. I told him that and as a consequence he had a very nice ceremony. I remember the funeral people made her look very pretty. She was very pretty lying in her coffin. She was a pretty woman. She was interred in the mausoleum along with my father.

I think as a result of the speech the rabbi gave, my brother Manny suggested after the ceremony that we get back together. After my mother's funeral, riding in the same limousine, Manny said, "You know what, why don't we forget the past?" and we began to see each other. We traveled together a number of times, on cruises. We had a short period of time to try to get our families together and we took a couple of cruises with our families. Later we took a few cruises with Manny and Barbara, about three or four. We went to Acapulco and also to Alaska. We tried to have a good time. It was deliberate, not off hand. It was a polite association. Later it became a more difficult situation because Manny got sick and eventually I couldn't understand what he was saying. He was aggravated at having to have his wife communicate what he was saying because she understood him. I had to turn away from him to look at Barbara. He would be standing to one side.

Cruising with Manny and Barbara 1989

I regret the split from my brother. After we got back together it wasn't long before he developed Parkinson's disease and it became difficult to talk and our communication dwindled. It became more of a relationship with his wife Barbara. Sadie and I have had many long lasting reciprocal relationships. I know Nick and Barbara were glad to get together again but I am sorry about the long split. Because of the 20 year split, I don't know my nephews, Gregory and Nick, very well. My mother and Sadie never really reconciled. My mother continued to challenge my allegiance by creating choices I would have to make between herself and Sadie.

We have connected with Russian relatives over the years. When the daughters of my mother's sister Branchik (Brenda in English), Itka's twin, and their children and spouses came over from Russia to New York a few years ago, we visited the family there and enjoyed a big dinner with them. I made a connection between Gary Alderson, my niece Neva's husband, and Alex, who is the husband of Eva, Branchik's granddaughter. They were both electrical engineers and Gary managed to get Alex a job with his company in Michigan. Alex and Eva were friends with Neva and Gary. The guys turned out to be very much alike and enjoyed playing tennis together. Neva and Eva are both named after my mother's mother, Eva, or Yeva, or Hava.

Sadie and I visited relatives in Russia and Mexico. We have been in contact with, and entertained other relatives such as my mother's nephew, Joseph (the son her oldest brother Leo), who immigrated to the Los Angeles area in the '80s.

When my brother, Manny, was dying, it was also bewildering to me because I felt I was a stranger. Although our animosity was long gone, I was treated as an outsider. No one asked me for any advice. My family was expecting Barbara to have some kind of service in his memory but she didn't. I wasn't angry with her because it's quite a traumatic experience.

My parents had the whole arrangement made in advance. Usually they just have people say nice things. I was supposed to say something at my father's funeral but I got up there and I couldn't talk. I wanted to have a rabbi at my mother's funeral although she had not made those arrangements.

I made my own arrangements in the '70's. I thought ahead. You can't predict your death. I could afford to do it and thus protected my kids from some burdensome bills. I feel because cremation leaves little evidence of an individual's existence, if you feel like remembering them on a memorial day, there's no place to visit.

Before those last days, however, we were talking about personal subjects. My mother was 89 or 90; sick in the hospital. She confessed to me an unrepeatable personal falsehood. A lot of women lie about their age. We spoke of contention between myself, her and Manny. Some communication took place, in regard to her consulting Manny about a loan involving interest paid by me to her at a good rate. I had to get a loan to buy my condominium in Beverly Hills. I figured, she had her money in a Savings and Loan at four and a half per cent. I had to pay seven and a quarter per cent for the loan. I told her, if she wanted to, I could get the loan from her and pay her the seven and quarter per cent. She said she'd think about it. About a week later, I had to make a decision; either get the loan from her or from the bank. She said, "Well, I've decided not to do that." I went ahead and got the bank loan and bought the condominium but I asked her "How come?" and she said that she had talked it over with Manny and he had advised against it. I said, "Well, that's very funny because you asked him if you should loan me money but you didn't ask me if you should sell a house to him!" She said, "Well, what business was it of yours?"

I had helped them buy in the first place, by loaning my folks the profits from my first real estate transaction. It was their business although I felt left out because I was the only other son. This was something that was very personal and I should have been told. I didn't have to be involved in the decision but I should have been told. They never told me until after the fact. I was upset simply being a member of the family and not being told what was what. My mother acted as though she realized a connection she hadn't seen before. She realized that she did play Manny against me or me against him. This was in her late eighties. She did realize it because she said "Oh my!"

I don't think she realized how serious what she was doing was. She didn't realize the discrepancy. It's a matter of family tradition like money or inheritance. She did not involve me in one thing and she involved Manny in the other. It was a terrible discrepancy. There was no communication. It was pretty obvious that what she was doing was against me. She was accomplishing what she wanted to do. She wanted to hurt me and she did. I made her face it. She did what she wanted without realizing the consequences. Now she opened a can of worms. Why was Manny to be consulted in one regard and not me in another? What also hurt that she blamed Manny for her decision. She did not want to be the one to make the decision. I don't know that she even consulted Manny. I think she was capable of either side.

I think she began to feel guilty that she mistreated me. I knew she was in a bad situation and I was visiting her every day. I didn't carry a grudge.

It's not easy to be negative about your mother. I try to see the situation from her point of view: she was angry and hurt because I "abandoned" her by running off and marrying Sadie. She then tried to punish me. She split me from Manny. My mother did not try to reconcile her sons. She also may have been afraid of competition: that Sadie and Barbara might become friends. She could have done something. She didn't consider the consequences of her actions. Women don't always think things through.

My mother "thawed out," realizing that I was taking time out of my day to visit her, for a period of about a year. After that conversation, our relationship became more personal. We talked. I visited her more because I wanted to than out of a sense of duty. She needed that. Nobody was left. She lived to be 90 years old. There was no one else close enough to visit her except me and Manny. Our duty was obvious.

Chapter 16: The Mail Delivery Business

The mail delivery business works like this: a company wanted its mail as early as possible. The way a postal route is laid out, the carrier starts at the beginning and goes to the end. It depends on where the company is on the route at what time it gets its mail. If you happen to be at the end of the route, you get your mail at 2:00 p.m., but you want it at 8:00 a.m. The businesses would have a Post Office box and they would have to send an employee to the Post Office to get their mail.

I said, "I can pick up your mail and deliver it to you cheaper than you can." So, they said, "Okay." I wasn't asking for money, but conducting a survey. I would get an audience. I got some very encouraging answers. Some of the people would say, "If it's going to save me some money, yeah, I'd be interested, how much are you going to charge?" I'd say "$15 a month." "They'd say, "Well, that's not very much money." I'd say, "Less than half a pizza a day!"

I had a feeling that I had a market for it. I decided to go into business. At the end of January, 1953, I went to talk to Bill Green, the Superintendent of Mail, and told him that I had decided to quit. At mid January I had gone back to the people who had expressed interest in private mail delivery. Out of those in North Hollywood who said they would be interested, five said, "Yeah, I could start February 1." My first customer was Glendale Federal Savings and Loan, a commercial venture, on Ventura Blvd. in Studio City.

When I started the mail delivery business in '53, I was taking a big risk. My father went into the bloomer business in Philadelphia in 1929 with his friend and they went broke. Manny had a good job and didn't need to take a big risk. It didn't occur to me to ask him to join me in the venture. It had been two years since we had tried the business as a side line for extra money.

I had a very good reputation in the Post Office. Bill Green had a brother-in-law at the Post Office who was a carrier who didn't want to be a mailman much longer. Bill promoted him to Superintendent when the Pico Heights station opened up. He promoted me to go with his brother-in-law as Assistant Superintendent because with me his brother-in-law could run the Post Office. Without me, he couldn't. As a carrier, he didn't know what goes on inside the Post Office. I was in charge of the clerical and another Assistant Superintendent was in charge of the carriers. When I decided to quit, Bill Green was sorry to see me go because I was the right hand man for his brother-in-law. Anyway, he told me something that he didn't tell anybody else. He said, "Okay, go ahead. But if anything goes wrong, if you made a mistake, you come back here and I'll put you right back where you were." That was the best kind of a back-up I could possibly get. I was "on leave." As a postal employee I could always come back. For example, if I spent 17 years in the Post Office, I had 17 years of return. That was the rule. But your return would depend on if there were a vacancy, and you had to start at the bottom.

In the Post Office you accumulated money for your retirement. The Post Office automatically put in money for you on a regular basis. After 17 years I had $1,000. I had a right to claim it, or borrow on it. So I claimed the money but it wasn't enough to buy a delivery van and have money to live on. My brother-in-law Chuck, Mae's husband, the accountant, took me to the Bank of America and they loaned me the money to buy a truck and he signed for me, because I had no established credit. I found an ad in the paper for the vehicle I was looking for. It was a tan truck or van, a prelude to the station wagon. I bought it from a musician who used to haul his instruments in it for his band. We could live on the $1,000 while I tried out the new business. I had an artistic neighbor, a woman who was an artist of a sort, paint "Universal Mail Delivery Service" on the truck. I started out and worked very hard. I didn't mind because it was exciting.

In 1953, we charged $15.00 a month. I would deliver the mail to my customers in the morning, come home, change clothes and go out soliciting for more customers. Then I would come home, change clothes and make an afternoon mail delivery to customers who were paying for two deliveries a day. When I had enough customers in the North Hollywood Area, I started soliciting in Burbank for more customers. When I had enough customers in Burbank, I bought another truck. It was a yellow truck and the same woman who was an artist painted "Universal Mail Delivery Service" on it. Sadie was driving the tan van, I was driving the yellow van.

Sadie did the deliveries in North Hollywood. The second truck I got through a loan from a bank. Before long I had four or five routes. After Burbank I solicited in Glendale, Van Nuys and then Beverly Hills. After Beverly Hills I went back to North Hollywood because things change, new businesses arrive, old businesses close up.

I was running the mail delivery service out of my house. In the evening we started picking up outgoing mail around 4:00 and were through by 6:00. When I was out soliciting during the day I would do both noon runs. I kept the trucks at the gas station where I bought my gas, about a block away.

Soon I had enough business to need outside help. I hired postal people from Terminal Annex whom I had known as fellow employees who needed extra income and could work a shift for me between their shifts. Sometimes people I hired would tell other postal employees. The Post Office was always at least two years behind the general public as far as pay was concerned. They were always fighting to try to catch up. They never really accomplished that. So if you wanted anything extra, like a radio or a TV (which was then brand new on the market), you had to find an extra job for a couple of hours so you could make the payments. If, when the payments were done, you wanted to quit, you could. Or maybe you decided to keep working extra hours to get something else. It was difficult to make ends meet and usually both the husband and wife worked somewhere.

If a guy went to work at 5:00 at night he could work a morning shift for me. The carrier who went to work in the morning and got off at 2:00 in the afternoon could do a night run for me. My first five or more employees were from the Post Office. I paid 75 cents an hour, a good rate then. Most places paid 50 cents.

This was an exciting time for me; it was productive. I went out, and I would get business. It wasn't anything tiresome or useless. I was developing a business which had a good market. My service was needed. It was so much simpler for the companies to have me pick up their mail and deliver it to them than to have their employees do it. I was picking up one or two new accounts every week. It went very well but I worked very hard. Meanwhile we were living on the $1,000. We spent as little as possible. I had to manage the money very carefully.

I was working very hard establishing a business and didn't have much of a home life. In the beginning I would get up about 6:00 a.m. The mail was available about 7:00. I was through about 5:30 p.m. I would have dinner and watch TV a little bit, but I would have to be in bed by 10:00 because I would have to be up at 6:00 again. I was not involved with the kids and their homework. That was Sadie's department. During the first years of starting the business we didn't have a social life.

I would teach someone a route and I would do a new route. We put our youngest son Bob in a pre-school while Sadie did the North Hollywood route. I replaced Sadie with an employee before long. It took us about five employees before we made any money, about a year, because we had to use the profits to pay the employees. The business was growing fast. We had to keep shoving routes onto other employees. I spent more time soliciting than doing the routes.

After a while I knew who to call on as potential customers and who to leave alone, who to pursue and who to forget. I was able to determine who really needed my services. If they do, I'm going to really stick to them; if they don't, I won't. There's no sense in wasting time.

In fact, there is one customer we still have today after 50 years. They make airplane parts. The man who ran the Company mail room wanted my service. He had to get permission from the controller and it was the furthest thing from the controller's mind. He wasn't interested in the mail. I called on Schroeder, who ran the mail room, for a year. He knew what the mail room expenses were and what the problems were.

The company had a station wagon and there was a girl that was one of his employees in the mail room and he sent her to the Post Office every day with that station wagon. Sometimes she would call in sick. So now he was all bewildered because somebody had to go get the mail. Sometimes they sent someone who didn't have the authority with the Post Office to pick up mail. For example, when we got a customer, they had to say "It's okay to release the mail to Universal Mail Delivery Service" and they had to sign it and that became the authority for the Post Office to give the mail to Universal Mail. So no matter who we sent, he was authorized when he identified himself as a Universal employee. That wasn't the case with Schroeder. This girl was authorized and if somebody else went there, they wouldn't give them the mail. So he had a lot of problems with it, on top of which was that what I charged them was about half of what they were paying for insurance on that car.

One day I said to him, "Maybe I ought to talk to your boss?" He says to me, "Be my guest!" So I called the boss up to make an appointment. It was set up for Tuesday. Tuesday morning his secretary calls me up to cancel. I said, "Well, can I make another appointment?" She says, "Well, come next week." The following Tuesday she called again and canceled. He was trying to get rid of me. But I knew they needed me. So, finally, he gets on the phone and says, "You come in this afternoon at 2:00. So I came in. He said, "You're a goddamn pest! You're wasting my time!"

I said, "In the first place, I'm more concerned about my time than your time. Not only do I not want to waste my time, but I don't think I'm wasting it! I can save you a lot of money and do your company a lot of good!" He was sort of taken aback at that. I told him, "If I thought you couldn't use my service, I would not be wasting my time."

He said, "Okay, I'm going to give you a contract for one month. You screw up once and you're out." I said, "Okay."

He called Schroeder in and he set it up. One month. He's still with us, fifty years later. Schroeder knew that our service would be way cheaper and more efficient for them. They have been our longest tem customer. They never have to worry about their mail.

We also provided courier services to our customers. Glendale Federal Savings, our first customer, had an advertising campaign where they glued two shiny pennies on the ad. There was a saying: "For two cents, I'd knock your block off," or some such thing. Glendale asked me to deliver the pennies to the printing office where they made their ad. I had this small truck and I put the bags of pennies on it and the truck sank. There were a lot of white canvas bags full of pennies! Maybe 500 pennies in each one. I loaded up the whole shipment and I couldn't move the truck because the bed sank down on the wheels and on the springs. So I took the bags of pennies off until the bed lifted up and I made two trips.

The courier service was part of the Universal Mail Delivery business. Glendale Federal began opening branches and we became their courier. It is different than mail delivery in that you don't deal with the Post Office. When I started with Glendale Federal in '53 they only had two offices, one in Studio City and one in Glendale. As time progressed they kept opening new offices. By the time they had fifteen I was couriering for them. I had a good relationship with the manager of the Studio City office, my first customer. The main office in Glendale would call him and say, "Hey, can you get somebody to do this and that?" He'd say, "Sure." After we had been delivering the mail awhile, somebody called him and said, "Could you get someone to deliver the pennies?" He didn't know if I could or couldn't, but he started with me. I had been delivering his mail regularly for three or four or five months.

I would pick up stuff from the head office in Glendale and deliver it to all the branch offices. Then I would pick up stuff, paperwork, from the branch office and deliver it back to the head office. We were "on-call" for anything they wanted delivered. "Can you do this? Can you do that? "Yeah, I can do anything, as long as you're willing to pay for whatever it takes to do it." This was custom delivery. The driver who delivered the items would get a signature on a bill, bring it into our office and it got filed under the customer's account. At the end of the month we would look in the file and bill for all the extras.

Developing a Business

Developing a business is like doing a jigsaw puzzle. Every time a new customer came in, that was a new "tile" that you had to find a spot for. For example, you've got thirty routes and a new customer comes in. What route do you give it to? When a business grows, it grows one puzzle piece at a time. A picture isn't painted until you've painted it, and a business isn't built until you've done the work. My hard work was done. When I started out, I'd get up at 6 in the morning and wouldn't have dinner until after 7. I put in 12, 13, 14-hour days. When my sons came in to run the business, they thought that how I was working at that time was all there was to it. When Marvin took over the warehouse situation, it was like, "Okay, I've got an office, I've got a manager. I'm going fishing." It wasn't like that. You have to keep your eye on things. After I got back from a trip, knowing that Murphy was taking care of things, the first thing I did was put myself back and forward to know what happened while I was away. You have to know the business from top to bottom. You can't depend on someone else to do your job.

When I came back, information was on my desk, new customers that came in or whatever it was, as it happened. That's the way I wanted it, because Murphy or anybody else could forget to tell me what happened. I was involved in the process of building the business, where my sons Bob and Marvin were given the business. They had no involvement with building it from the inside out like I did. They thought it was a snap because they were already on top. The next thing you know they went broke because they think the guy they appointed to run their business is going to do the job for them. He can't; he doesn't know how.

The services, like the delivery of the pennies, would all go on the bill at the end of the month. I did my own billing. I would come in on

Saturday. There were no computers then. I didn't get a computer until sometime in the early '70's. I did it on a typewriter. I knew exactly how the business was doing. By the time we got computers, 20 years after I started the business, we had about 30 trucks running. We managed the routes from the home office. We would print out a route at first, when we had a change we would give the driver a new print out, with the changes highlighted. The driver would come to work in the morning and pick up an empty truck. He would go to the Post Office, pick up the mail and lay it out, in his truck, in sequence to be delivered.

He would get the courier stuff from our office in the morning when he picked up the mail, because it had been picked up from the customer the night before. We had a morning crew and a night crew. We stayed open from 4:00 in the morning to 10:00 at night.

If I had thirty trucks, I probably had 60 employees. We had one office. Eight people worked in the office. I did both managing and sales. By then I had an office manager who ran the office. That was my friend, the former Postal Inspector, Murphy. He made it possible for me to go on trips.

The business wasn't intimidating; it was challenging! Customers kept asking us, "Could you do this for us?" For example, "Could you make a bank deposit for us?" "Sure, we can make a deposit." We didn't have insurance to cover money, so we worked based on that information. No insurance company would cover money. Stock brokers had insurance for money. They put us on their insurance policy. The money was always checks. They were in small canvas bags with zippers. The banks trusted your insurance. When the insurance companies found out what was going on, they wouldn't allow it any more unless we were really employees. We told them ahead of time that we did not handle cash.

What happened at that time was that bonds were "bearer" bonds. Your name wasn't on there; anybody could steal it and have it. (Today they don't do that. You don't get a bond; you get a letter saying that you bought the bond, describing the bond. It isn't legal tender.) There was one robbery. It was by one of our own drivers. We were doing an inter-office delivery for one of the stock brokers. Some negotiable bonds disappeared. The driver hid them under the carpet of his living room. He figured he could leave them there for a month or two and then cash them.

We knew he did it — he was the only one who could have possibly done it, although he claimed he lost it. Well, there were detectives involved. They noticed that the rug in his house was not flat. It had lumps in it. They lifted up the carpet and there were the bonds! The driver had to go to jail. That was the only robbery we had. Thieves are often stupid, leaving all kinds of evidence behind them.

We developed several innovations in Post Office procedures through Universal Mail Services. The North Hollywood Post Office was very cooperative. The Postmaster realized that we helped them. I created some Post Office forms that had to be approved by Washington and they were because they saved the Post Office a lot of money. This happened early on. It was a pretty obvious problem. You simply had to solve it. An example of an innovative procedure we developed is the "Postage Due" advice form. If we had a dozen or so customers, our driver had to carry money with him and we had to make a list of who had what. It was time-consuming. I created a list of our customers and I gave it to the Post Office. I also gave the Post Office a deposit of $100. They deducted the Postage Due from my deposit. They also gave me a Postage Due slip that my driver gave to the bookkeeper so that it could be added to each customer's bill. The Postage Due form became very handy on the computer because when the driver came in he entered who owed how much. Every time you have a problem you have to think of a solution.

Our biggest Post Office pick up was Van Nuys. (Now it's Thousand Oaks of all places. Nobody lived there when we started. Now everybody's moving out in that direction.) We had about 4 routes out of Van Nuys. We organized the routes by color. They had cases at the

Post Office with the different colors which made our routes easier to indentify. This was called a "Phantom Post Office Box" or "caller service." It was just a number, not an actual Post Office box.

I would do the original delivery in a new territory. When it got to be five or six accounts, I would hire someone from the Post Office to make the deliveries and I would go to another territory. Five years after I started Universal Mail, I could afford a vacation in Hawaii in 1958 for our 25th wedding anniversary.

I had developed the business quickly.

Chapter 17: Sav-On Freight

A few months after I started the mail delivery service, I got the idea for Sav-On Freight while soliciting business for the Mail Delivery Service from a toy company. He started telling me about the freight problem. He told me about the system of the "advance." I had to really look into it. I called a trucking company and they gave me answers to my questions. There was interest. I got home and thought about it and it seemed like a good idea.

The rules of the freight game were that if you got something that the Post Office couldn't handle, being too big or whatever, the cost of freight from one point to another was a minimum for 100 pounds. In other words if you had a shipment of 35 pounds they would charge you for 100. The idea was to get the shipper to consolidate his customer's freight in my area and send it to me. I would do the distribution. It was consolidated freight distribution. The shipment was consigned to my company, Sav-On Freight. Sav-On Freight distributed the freight to the buyer of the stuff.

I got involved in the shoe business. I told my brother-in-law Chuck about the freight consolidation business and he said that shoe stores have that problem. When they place an order, it's usually 35 or 40 pounds. The shoe industry had four trade shows a year at that time. Chuck told me about their show in L.A. and suggested that that would be a good place to start.

I went up there and explained how this idea worked, talking to each stall. Those that thought it was a good idea tried it out and "Deb" shoe was the first one. I had a flyer which I had printed. I developed a procedure during the show. Questions came up that led to procedures and solutions. For example, I would need a manifest form telling me what was being shipped, as well as address labels to be used on the shipment directing it to me. Then I created a delivery receipt which I would give to the driver and would ultimately get back, signed by the recipient of the freight. I got the procedure developed quickly and the forms produced which I carried around with me when I was talking to potential shippers at the industry show.

I talked to the salesman for "Deb" shoes who was at the show. He thought I had a good idea and suggested that I write to the shipping manager of his company. So I did, explaining the procedure.

This is how it worked. You had a store and you had a 35-pound shipment coming. Another store has a 35-pound shipment coming in from the same source. One store was in North Hollywood, two stores in Los Angeles, etc. I would write a letter to the shoe company and tell them that if they would consolidate and send their shipment to me, I would deliver it to their customers. I went back to the shoe company in St. Louis to try to tell them how to save money for their customers without costing them anything by consolidating their freight with me.

For example, say I had three customers at 35 pounds each which is 105 pounds. I pay shipping for 105 pounds, at $10 per 100 pounds. I charge the customer $3.50 for a 35-pound shipment, which I had paid for them in advance; $ .50 for service charge, so that's $4.00. The delivery charge from my dock to the customer is $2.00; so a total of $6.00 is better than $10.00, a savings of $4.00 to the customer and I made $1.50 on it. The customer would write the manufacturer that he would like his goods delivered to Sav-On Freight. The return for me was in the volume of freight delivered. The customers told other shoe companies and that increased my business. At four deliveries, I made $2.00, each customer saving money in the process. To keep track of what goes where, the shipper would send me what is called a manifest. On the manifest it would say how much freight there was and who the consignees (my customers) were. With that information I created a delivery receipt for the delivery carrier. I did the book work. At first I did it on Bellingham in my house but somebody complained. The neighbors didn't like having big trucks coming down the road delivering freight to my house. I kept the freight in my garage during the day and Twentieth Century Trucking came and picked up the freight every night to be delivered in the morning. As the business increased, there were more and more trucks.

I moved the business to a storefront at 7450 Lankershim in September of '53 to run both businesses. The store became my office. It was the cheapest thing I could find. I remember this truck drove up with some freight for us. I didn't have cash on hand to pay for the bill. I wanted to either write a check or have him bill me. So the driver called up his main office to see if it was okay to leave the freight. He's talking to the office and I hear him say, "It's some rundown hole-in-the-wall over here." That was pretty funny! It was a store front, but it was long and narrow.

In the meantime I had to develop a procedure that could work. I would send the shipper a bunch of labels that said, "Deliver to Sav-On Freight at such and such an address in North Hollywood." I would pay the delivery charge which was an advance to my customers, which was collected along with my fee and the Century Truck delivery fee. I would make up the delivery receipts and I would hire 20th Century Trucking to send a truck over to pick up the freight and make the deliveries. The delivery receipt was in triplicate. I would keep a copy, give one to the delivery man who would sign it, and he would give one to the shipment recipient. The delivery truck would collect the advance together with my fee on the outbound and send me back their copy along with the money, which was handled by the bookkeeper at 20th Century Trucking.

Every business has its own esoteric language. In the freight business there are terms like manifest, advance, inbound, distribution, and consolidation. These words are pretty much confined to the delivery business. The "advance" is an intra-trucking feeless COD. By using this method of collecting my money it was possible to continue in this business.

In this way I got paid; I got my advance returned (which I had paid on the inbound), and evidence that the goods had been delivered. I would back file in duplicate. This would keep me informed. They would keep their delivery charge. I had to hire a trucking company because the mail trucks weren't big enough. It became cumbersome. I kept the Universal Mail Service business separate.

I solicited for the Sav-On Freight business by sending out letters and also visiting retail industry shows. I would tell them how I could save them money through consolidated freight. This was a new idea at the time. I started with the shoe business. Later on I got involved with all kinds of businesses: greeting cards, clothing, toys, everything. If you had packages, we were in. The idea is that there are changes out there all the time over which you have no control. It is a desirable situation in business to be diversified and to have business reserves. For example when the Teamsters went on strike, nobody delivered any freight. I had to pay my office staff even though I didn't have any money coming in. I depended on my reserves.

After I started Sav-On Freight I opened an office in Oakland. I had a friend from the Post Office, Ray Smart, who had started a mail delivery service with a partner in Oakland. Ultimately his partner bought him out. Ray came to work for me in L.A. We had been friends for a long time. Fate crossed our paths innumerable times. I knew him when I worked for my father in the chicken store. He and his father-in-law came to buy chickens for his father-in-law's store. Several years later, we found out that we were working at the Post Office together and became friends, back around '36 or '37. We were friends socially at the Post Office, for example, in the Post Office bowling league or Post Office picnics.

He needed my expertise in order to know how to run a mail delivery service. He wasn't in competition with me in Oakland. So we kept in touch. When I decided to open Sav-On Freight in Oakland, he recommended his former partner, Ed, who could get the freight, break it down and deliver it up there. I referred to it as my Oakland Office, although it was his dock. They were making money off the deliveries. The freight was delivered to their dock. They didn't have to pick up the freight. They had a dock and an office. However the paperwork was done in L.A. He ran it for maybe a year.

The Bay area got more and more freight and it made sense economically to move the office to San Francisco. Ray Smart went up to run it because his friend wasn't really in the freight delivery business. He was in mail delivery. As the freight volume increased, it became too much for him to handle.

I bought a warehouse on 3rd street in San Francisco and sent Ray up. I planned to open a mail delivery service there as well. After Sav-On Freight was going for about a month, I went up there to check out the possibility of a mail delivery service. I found out that there was one outfit doing mail delivery, a man and his son, and they were doing one pick up in the morning. I could offer full service, morning, noon and night. I called on maybe 50 companies and 22 ultimately said yes. Two or three said okay for that week. I went up about once a month and followed up on the ones that were interested and the ones that had signed up. I was public relations and Ray was operations. We hired help.

Both companies got too big not to be in conflict. For example, you have one truck. Who gets the delivery first? The customer suffers and ultimately you suffer because you lose the customer. I decided to sell off Universal Mail in San Francisco to a competitor. I also sold the building and moved the operation onto Merchant Delivery's dock. I moved Ray down south and moved another employee up to San Francisco.

This employee, Bud, had been working for me for about two years in the General Office. I trusted him because he impressed me. He was religious, had a wife and two children and he seemed to have integrity. He ran the business off Merchant's Delivery Dock. About 6 months later the owner of Merchant's Delivery called me and said I would have to join the union or not be on his dock. So I rented another place, another dock, and at the same time decided to approach another union. By joining the other union which represented office workers, I negotiated a much better deal primarily because I volunteered to join and they didn't have to go after me. Once you're unionized, the other unions don't bother you.

Bud ran the show. He ran it well. There was enough there for him to steal without me feeling the theft. Not infrequently, freight is refused by the consignee for various reasons. We notify the shipper and await instructions. Most of the time, the shipper would tell us to ship it back, which we did and collected our charges as an advance. Sometimes the shipper would decide that the merchandise cost less than the cost of shipping it back. So they would abandon it. After accumulating this stuff, you would call in a dealer who would buy it up and get it out of your way. I would get the money back that I had invested in the shipping costs. Bud would sell the merchandise on his own, not reporting it as revenue. I had thought that because he was a churchgoing guy, that he was honest. Somewhere down the line, the devil got to him.

In the meantime, we had a New York customer who shipped his publication to us by air and we delivered it to the L.A. area stock broker subscribers. When they found out that we were in San Francisco they asked us to do the same there. One of Bud's jobs was to do that. That was early in the morning before he opened up Sav-On Freight. About a year later, our New York customer, called us and cancelled service out of San Francisco. After making some inquiries, we found out that Bud had offered to do the same work for a quarter less per delivery. He had begun working independently, doing the delivery before he came into our office. Something came up and I called up there to talk to Bud and one of the other workers said, "Well, Bud isn't here right now. He's delivering Dow Jones."

When I went up there to fire him face to face, I found out he was stealing typewriters. He wouldn't notify a customer if there was an overage in the delivery. Somewhere down the line, a claim would be made. I would have to pay the claim. When I went up there with my list of inventory, there was nothing there. I told Bud, "I'm sorry, I no longer need your services. You better take your things and go." I stayed up there a few days until Ray or Marvin could get up there. There were several people working there but I didn't know them well enough to put anyone in charge. Bud knew the score. You can't hang on to an employee that's stealing from you. It's easy to fire someone when you're in the right.

I found out a lot of things after I fired Bud. He was doing it before he went to work for me. They think "I'm doing it all." They don't realize that I have overhead. They find justification in doing things like that. Any business needs capital. The money that is saved by the owner/managers is used for growth, creating more jobs and is also used for emergencies. A business does not go on and on without incidents. There are good times and bad times. When the bad time comes you have to have enough capital saved up to accommodate your needs. Unfortunately, many employees think that management is taking too much money out of the pot and that they should get more of the money than they're getting.

I was a big customer of a trucking company called Western Car Loading. They shipped railroad carloads of freight which they unloaded on arrival here in L.A. and routed it for local delivery. Whatever freight I had, they delivered to me on my dock. I gave it to 20th Century for local delivery. Western Car Loading assigned a salesman to me here in L.A. When I was in New York I went to visit Western Car Loading and they always made sure that they entertained me. They would take me to lunch and we would talk business. I was a thinker and always had ideas about business development that would benefit both of us.

At one of these nice lunches at a New York private business club, we discussed the fact that I wanted a salesman on the East Coast to help build my business in the cosmetic industry. The Vice President of Western Car said it just so happened that a good friend of his, Sammy Zipkin, was in the freight business. He had decided to close his business and was looking for something to do. Perfect timing. My friend took me to Sammy's business office on 39th street and we sat down and talked. Sammy knew what I was talking about and we agreed that he would be my East Coast Representative. He kept his office until the lease ran out and then we got a new office. His office was too big, having been in the delivery business for himself. You have to be a good salesman if you're in business for yourself.

Because I was a good customer of Western Car Loading, it was to their benefit for me to have a good salesman. The more business I had, the more I would give to them. Sammy had been in the trucking business for a while in New York. The trouble with being in business in New York is that graft is not deductible. Payoffs to the police and unions were so great that by the time he reported his income, taxes took the rest. When he started losing money to that extent, he decided to close his business. I was not subject to that type of corruption because all I needed was a salesman who could operate from his home if he wanted. We opened a nice office on Broadway in an office building (when Sammy's lease ran out) because it gave us a credible presence which was good for sales.

Sammy was a New Yorker and like New Yorkers, he talked rough. Sammy knew how to handle the people in New York City. He was one of them. He did very well for us. Sammy would have our customers send their stuff to Western Car Loading. They had their own security set-up. I didn't know or care what it was. They were open twenty-four hours. I was their customer.

Our office on Broadway was near a building of individual wholesale showrooms where business competitors displayed their wares as an industry. Down the street might have been another building representing a different product or industry such as children's clothes. These buildings were all over Manhattan. When they had their seasonal shows, maybe for one week each, buyers would come out from the West Coast. Sammy would show them how to ship for less. Eventually he would visit the factories. It's easier to do business with someone you know rather than someone you don't know. He would make sure that everything was being done properly in shipping so that the maximum benefit would be the result. He would go to North and South Carolina, Massachusetts, Georgia, Pennsylvania, New York itself. Pretty soon he covered that whole area.

I gave Sammy a good salary to start with. When you're in business, you have to invest; I invested in Sammy. I told him that he would get a bonus based on sales. He did well. He got a good bonus. We became close. We had a good relationship. We knew his two boys all the time they were growing up. One of their sons, Danny, moved out here and would visit us sometimes. He was one of the owners of PCPI, the computer company that developed an aspect of the computer "mouse." They sold the patent and did very well. My daughter Barbara and Danny's wife were good friends.

Every once in a while I would go with him on these public relations visits. The shippers would welcome him. Sammy was a very nice man. He was a good salesman. He enjoyed being a salesman. He liked people. He had a sense of humor. He was fun. We used to go to New York just to be with Sammy and his wife, Ruth. I considered him a family member. Being close friends with an employee is a gamble, but with Sammy I won. Sammy Zipkin was a charismatic type of individual that I liked right away. He was not a phony.

We would go out to eat at special restaurants. He knew all the good ones. One time we met him in New York and from there the four of us drove to Boston, where we made several calls. On the way back we toured the New England area and since it was fall, we saw the wonderful changing color of the leaves.

Sammy and his wife, Ruth, would come to L.A., where I put them up in a hotel. He knew everyone at the L.A. office. We had about twelve office workers in the office in Vernon, mostly women, and about twelve men on our docks at the same location.

Sammy's visit was mostly social. I would take him down to Ninth Street in L.A. where he would meet the salespeople of the factories that he visited back East. It would create a bond that would strengthen our business relationship.

At one time or another every shipper in the United States used our services. Eventually we got competition. They didn't do it as systematically as we did. I would do the paperwork on Saturdays or Sundays. I worked seven days a week. After a while Sav-On Freight became a big business, with 30 people working for me. There is a reason why some people succeed in business. It takes hard work and a desire to do the hard work. The product you're selling, service or goods, has to have some value. You have to keep investing, with an eye on the future. You have to build reserves so that you're not dependent on your investment.

There are different levels of business development from the small business, say a push cart peddler, to the multi-billion dollar corporation. Let's say we divide business into 5 sectors, 5 being the biggest. I was at level 3. I saw a problem with going bigger in the difficulty of obtaining good management. People either don't want to manage, or can't because they don't understand management. It's not easy. For, one thing, they're afraid to tell people what to do because they want to be pals with everybody. Being a manager means you can't be pals with everybody.

One of the most important parts of running a business is collecting the money that's due you. All bills are paid reluctantly. Nevertheless, most are paid. Every Sunday I would write letters to people who had not paid their bill, reminding them they owed me money. I gave them plenty of time to pay. There was one person who was very argumentative. It was a pretty heavy argument. He realized that he was saving money using my service. He realized that his company was big enough to pay the bills. He realized that I can't afford to pay his bills. Some of the big companies took advantage of you by making you wait 90 days instead of paying the bill on a monthly basis. If you wanted their business you had to wait 90 days. I said "I don't need a customer who doesn't pay his bills." He got on the ball. He instructed his bookkeeping department to pay bills from Sav-On Freight right away. He became a most reliable payer.

Some of our customers only communicated to us with their traffic manager, the manager of the warehouse. He would say, "Look, I send the bill up there. If they don't pay, it's not my fault." I would say, "Well, okay, you can tell 'em that I need the money." He says, "Well, I can go up and tell 'em but it just goes in one ear and out the other. They'll pay you when they get around to it." I said, "In that case, I'll deliver your freight when I get around to it." The psychological factor of collecting money is that if you don't ask for it, they don't give it to you. They figure your profitability is so high you don't need it, otherwise you would be pressing for it. This is a big problem in any business. Get your money, because if you don't, every month you let go by without asking for it makes it harder for them because in the mean time they spend the money for something else. It's a business priority.

Between management and collections and everything else required to run a business, I found out that if you devote 8 hours to one business, you do just as well as devoting four and four to two businesses. You might just as well do it for one, it's much simpler. I found "you can't ride two horses at one time."

Computers

In 1979 we got computers and everything changed. It was "good business sense" to get computers. They said "If we put computers in, we can save hundreds of dollars on help." Not true; the more computers you have, the more help you need. Computers have some value and as time went on we grew into it but in the meantime you would spend money like crazy. Sure, it was expensive to convert but it was necessary.

Later, the routes were on the computers. If I wanted to see a route, I would just punch the route name in and everything would show up on the computer, telling me where the driver was, what he was doing, who the customers were, what time he was due there. But some things require a decision; not a computer decision, but a personal decision. The computer can tell you where the driver with the problem is. Now, you've got to get another driver to get out there and finish the route. Maybe another driver to bring him in; or you have to call a tow truck. I knew everything that was going on in the business.

Now there is a computer on every desk, upstairs and down. Whoever comes in off the routes enters whatever he needs to on the computer and it is accumulated upstairs. We have a computer specialist because we have to. The first computer was a total loss. I had to have a whole room for the machinery. At that time we had punch cards. One of the problems on the computer at that time was that if it broke down, you couldn't start it again where it broke down, you had to start it from the beginning. Okay, so I was running bills, the monthly bill for our customers. You got a thousand customers. The machine runs and runs and runs and when it hits the 600's, it breaks. I have to throw away all 600 bills because I can't start at 601. I can only start it at 1. It was very costly. I stopped using it.

It cost a fortune to put it in to begin with. I needed a room and an air conditioning system just for that room. If the temperature in that room changed by two degrees, the machine would go off and then start all over again. I sued the company. I had to take them to court and I got paid for all my problems. I didn't get another computer for quite a while. That computer was big as a counter top. The next computer was table top. In between, a lot had happened. In Van Nuys, we had six stations, running off one computer. Now, we can transfer information from one office to another through the computer over the Internet.

Chapter 18: Building a Business

By this time I had a manager for Universal Mail in Inglewood, where we had our main office, who used to be a Post Office Inspector, Jerry Murphy. Jerry had been an assistant for one of my competitors. Having been a postal inspector, he expected business to be run above board. He wasn't comfortable working for my competitor, so he came to me seeking a job. Jerry knew me through business association. We would go to lunches sponsored by the Postal Customer Council, PPC.

With me, Jerry became the President of the PPC for ten years. Anybody who wanted to communicate with the Post Office regarding any issue belonged to the PPC. The PPC was a national organization with local offices. Jerry was the Los Angeles president. I gave him the time and the money to go to Washington meetings. It was part of his job. It was good for business.

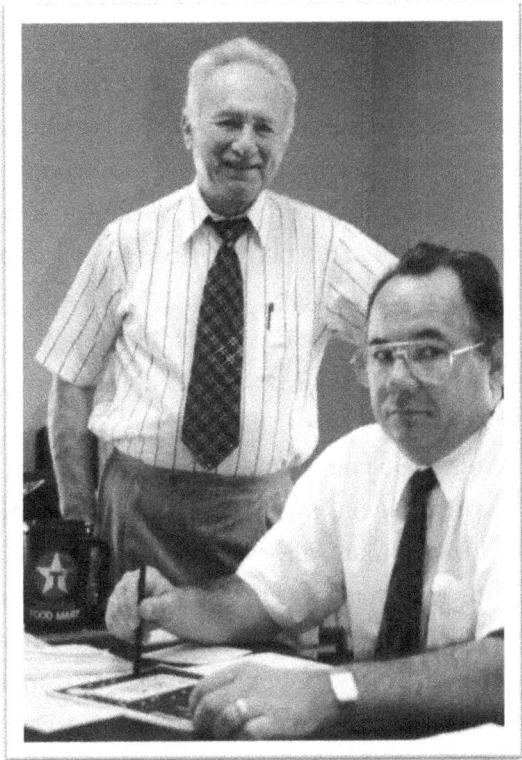

At work with my son, Marvin

Ultimately, because he was dependable, I depended on him to run the show when I traveled. This had become more and more frequent. We had a good relationship. We worked closely together, making business decisions together. We also socialized occasionally with our wives, going out to dinner. He was probably about twenty years younger. He worked for me for about twenty-six years. Jerry was looking forward to retirement, but unfortunately he died before he retired.

We had whatever we needed: secretaries and so forth. My brother-in-law Jerry, the accountant, kept the books and I checked them whenever I wanted to. I finally didn't do any of the bookwork. Jerry worked for me for about ten years before I got a CPA. I became the head salesman. The only one who really has an interest in building a business is the owner. No one else has the same motivation.

I was only at the Lankershim place for a short while, in '53 and part of '54, where I operated both Sav-On Freight and Universal Mail. From there I moved to a warehouse on Faire Avenue in North Hollywood. I was still operating both businesses out the same place. It had a big yard in a business district. There was also a Georgia Pacific Lumberyard on the same property. I had an office in the warehouse. By then I had about four trucks for Universal mail. I could park them in the yard. It was at this time that I built my house in the San Fernando Valley on Goodland in 1957.

About 1960 I moved to a nice office building in North Hollywood on Coldwater Canyon, which also had a big parking lot where I could park the Universal Mail Delivery trucks. By then I had about seven or eight blue trucks. While I was there, Murphy came to work for me. Eventually I arranged with the gas station/garage owner to park my trucks across the street at his Texaco gas station where I bought my gas. In the morning I paid one of the drivers to come in early and gas up the trucks so that when the other drivers came in they could simply drive off.

My trucks didn't interfere with his business because they were only parked there at night. The station was open all night and the garage

---

Home Design

In 1957, I built a new house on Goodland, in North Hollywood, where we lived until 1968. It was a very nice house. I had something to do with its construction and also with the architecture. When I looked at the plans I felt the design could be improved so I told the builder. He built two houses pretty much the same, selling me the lot as a package where he would build the house. I designed the pool around a palm tree. We had a kidney-shaped pool with a palm tree as an island.

When my son Bob bought a house in Pacific Palisades it was still under construction when he took me over there. I didn't like the design at all. The master bedroom was a small bedroom with a sliding door closet. The entryway was elaborate, big and wide. I said, "You know, you're wasting a lot of good space here. When you buy a house like this, the bedroom should have a walk-in closet. So I redrew the plan, narrowing the entryway by four feet, so you can imagine how big the entryway was. Instead of the sliding door closet in the bedroom that was one foot deep, I made a five foot deep walk-in closet. When the builder looked at it he said, "What a great idea!" and he changed all of the new houses to have that walk-in closet.

---

didn't do business at night so there was plenty of space. Because it was open all night it was more secure than the parking lot behind the office where we parked during the day. Once in a while someone would steal a battery or siphon off gas from the trucks at night at the office parking lot because it was dark and wide open.

Meanwhile I started using the docks (a place where the trucks can back into) of the delivery company, Brake Delivery Service, for Sav-On Freight. I had a couple of employees who reported to work directly at the docks. I would go over there several times a week to give them the manifest, which told them what to expect coming in and where it went.

In 1964 I bought a place in Inglewood and we moved the Mail Delivery Service to Inglewood. It was an acre with one building and several offices. The yard was plenty big for twenty-five trucks. You could probably put more than fifty trucks there. I put 25 trucks there and at the same time I bought a place in the valley which was at the end of Lankershim Boulevard and San Fernando Road. Murphy and I decided that we would split the territory. The Van Nuys office would handle everything for Universal Mail north of the Santa Monica Mountains. Inglewood handled everything south of the hills. I put thirty trucks in Inglewood. I put 25 in the Valley. By then we were full force. When people work for you, you're always looking for talent among them. You have to evaluate them: are they smart, do they care, do they use their head? You are always looking for people to promote into better positions to serve you and have them earn more money. In any business you want people to feel that there is a future, not a cul-de-sac. If there's no future, they are going to go somewhere else. If we saw a driver that showed intelligence and capability we would promote them to a managing position. We had to get a manager for the Valley.

We were operating Sav-On Freight off the Brake Delivery docks. The general office was combined with the Universal Office. Any business is divided into the general office and the operating office. I had two good men working on the Brake Delivery Docks. The paperwork went through the general office where it was processed. Each manifest was then accompanied by bills of lading for each delivery on the manifest. The bundle was then turned over to the men on the dock so that each delivery was accompanied by the necessary papers. My dock operator in charge of operations was Soto Armijo. He was with me a long time. He was reliable and I gave raises as warranted. There was a lot of inflation at the time. To keep help I had to keep up with the times.

We selected someone as manager for the Universal Mail Valley office, one of the drivers. At first he was okay but after two or three months, we noticed business wasn't expanding. We checked on the situation and discovered that he was turning business away. He didn't want to be bothered. He had a little more money now and he had started drinking. For whatever reason, he preferred the status quo. There is always a whistleblower because he needs to protect his own future. When you have a manager that doesn't allow a company to grow, it begins to shrink, and that's dangerous because you ultimately wind up without a job. It also affects employee morale. "Gee, this guy's getting paid for not doing his job." Customers move out of your service area. If there's no business coming in, business shrinks.

In 1967 I moved to a big, long, narrow warehouse in Vernon which had a lot of truck doors on one side. For the first time Sav-On Freight was operated independent of Universal. I operated Sav-On Freight and Murphy ran Universal. Truck doors are doors on the side of the building where the big trucks can back up and load or unload. On the other side of the building was a railroad spur, which was like an off ramp from the railroad track. The railroad engine would push or pull the railway car on or off the spur in back of my warehouse where there were doors to unload or load freight.

Here's the sequence. I started Sav-On Freight. I sent Marvin up there to San Francisco to run it up there. Then I sent Ray Smart. After Ray Smart, I sent Bud up there. While Ray Smart was there, we opened up Universal Mail Delivery up there. It wasn't getting anywhere because I didn't trust him and I didn't want to run to San Francisco every week. I had stuff to do here. So we decided to sell it. We sold Universal Mail Delivery Service, I sold the building, and I brought Ray down here. I sent Bud up there to run Sav-On Freight. In '76, UPS got ICC interstate rights. Although I had fired Bud beforehand and I had one of the other guys running it, I knew it was a losing proposition. I could see that it would never work. I decided to close Sav-On Freight. Everybody stopped shipping with us because UPS was more convenient.

I turned over the warehouse business that went with Sav-On Freight to my son Marvin. We warehoused for Olivetti typewriters. We did some warehousing for Sav-On Drugs and delivered the stuff when they needed it. When I closed it up in Vernon, Marvin went somewhere else and went into business for himself. He was still in Vernon but he wasn't in the same place with me. He got a bigger warehouse than we had. He started soliciting for warehouse business. He did very well the first year. It was the second year that he became a "big shot." He joined the L.A. Fish Club and let some other guy run the business, who ran it into the ground. The other guy hired people he didn't need. You have to watch that because labor is your highest cost. The second year, Marvin's business went downhill. Marvin wasn't paying attention. He let the other guy run it.

Chapter 19: Ray and Beezie

Ray Smart was with me for many years. He was a charismatic individual with personnel management capability. Because of his charisma he was able to get people to do what needed to be done in both businesses. Later we divided the functions of the main office. And later yet we divided the offices. I was always the boss of both.

In New York, Sammy generated business for Sav-On Freight all the way from Maine to Florida. I generated it from here. At that point I had a salesman for Universal Mail. When we had our 40th wedding anniversary surprise party for our guests on the Queen Mary, Ray and his wife had made the arrangements and were the receptionists for our group. They saw that the arrangements I had made were carried out. When we arrived at the ship he showed us where to go and everything went smoothly. He later started a mail delivery service in San Diego.

Ray Smart was a rogue. I would call him a charismatic rogue because of his mistreatment of women. He didn't mistreat friends. He was a womanizer to begin with and he took advantage of women. He was nice looking and got along well with everybody. If he did something bad, people would forgive him, even the women. He was easy to forgive. He was honest enough in a manner of speaking. He had four wives.

The first wife was Jewish and her kids all did very well without him. His daughter married a man in the cardboard carton business and they did very, very well. When Ray and his first wife, Francis, got married, they rented a small house trailer because that was the cheapest thing they could find during the Depression. They didn't even pay rent for the land because it was just an empty lot. We had just gotten out of high school. The newlyweds parked the trailer on an empty lot that happened to have a slight incline on its terrain. It was behind a factory that had a high brick wall. The trailer was kept stable by a couple of rocks behind the wheels. One night they were making love and they shook the trailer so badly that the rocks came dislodged and the trailer started rolling towards the brick wall and hit it with a big jar. That was one of his stories.

Then Ray married a Hispanic girl, Catholic, and had two kids with her. Nice girl but he took advantage of her. He went around with other women. She worked, so there was another income. He didn't pay that much attention to her and eventually they divorced. Their boy did well manufacturing surf boards in Hawaii.

After the Hispanic gal he married a black woman and they moved to Oakland. That's where he started the partnership with Ed, called Modern Mail Delivery. That broke up and when Ed bought him out he came to work for me, meanwhile divorcing the black woman. I had started Sav-On Freight so I got him involved in that. When I opened up an office in San Francisco I sent him up there.

Sadie had a friend, Beezie, a Methodist from Caspar, Wyoming. We were neighbors on Westhaven when they moved out here during the war. Sadie and Beezie became very friendly. Her husband, Earl, worked for the Pet Milk Company. He was a salesman. One day he said to me, "How's business?" I said, "Who cares?" I worked for the Post Office. Mail got delivered every day. I got paid every week. It was not an issue with me. Earl was struck by my answer. How could you not be concerned with how good or bad business is?

After a couple of years he was promoted to managing the sales office in Salt Lake City. Beezie and Sadie were so close that they would come down for a weekend and stay with Beezie's sister and visit Sadie also.

Earl did not understand bigotry against the Jews or why the Jews hated Hitler. He didn't understand the War really. I guess he didn't read the news. After all, Hitler was killing off a lot of people. I don't imagine there are a lot of Jews in Caspar, Wyoming. He didn't understand discrimination. However, he came back to Los Angeles from Salt Lake City because he found he was discriminated against there because he wasn't a Mormon. The first thing he did when he came back was to tell me, "Bernie, now I understand what discrimination is." If he went to a store and there was a competitive brand sold by a Mormon, they would buy that. He could make more money in L.A. as a salesman than he could in Salt Lake because he couldn't make any sales on the side and earn the commission. He found that his kids were discriminated against in school because they weren't Mormon.

Soon after we moved to the Valley in '49, they moved there also. Beezie was like a sister to Sadie. About five years later Earl suddenly committed suicide. No one knows why. He turned the engine on and sat in the car. We had known them for about ten years when Earl committed suicide. Beezie received insurance money but she still had two young children and had to do something. By then I was doing all right so I offered her a job, an interoffice run for Sears. It was about three hours in the afternoon, five days a week which suited her fine. Ray Smart was working for me on Coldwater in our general office. Ray and Beezie met and after a few years got married.

Ray was an Irishman with a lot of charisma, without too many religious values. He was a womanizer. He was my assistant. I knew him for many years and we were friends. However, he wasn't the best guy in the world as far as women were concerned.

When Beezie and Ray got married, she had the money from the insurance from the death of her husband. That was the nest egg he needed to start a mail delivery service in San Diego. They both quit their jobs with me and went to San Diego. Ray was not very smart business wise. He took nothing seriously.

He developed the business for five or six years and then sold it to somebody but the people were not happy. One day he disappeared and so did the bank account. He took the money and ran away. The divorce followed. They owned a house down there so she was able to mortgage it. She did fine without him.

He knew he did something bad because of our relationship with Beezie and I didn't see him. He forgave himself, though, and after a while would call me up and tell me what was going on, just to say hello. The next thing I know he's broke and house sitting in Palm Springs at the second home of his wealthy daughter who married the paper carton magnate. He had no expenses and could draw social security from when he worked for me. That's the last I heard of him.

Meanwhile he was already in his 70's. He used up Beezie's money. While I wasn't seeing him, he got sick. I didn't have anything to do with him businesswise or personally after that. It's not easy to break a relationship with someone with whom you've been friends with for about 25 years. He was with me in the Post Office for seventeen years.

Beezie still had the house they bought in San Diego and could collect social security again because she had turned 65. She had been receiving it after her husband died but lost it when she married Ray. She had two sons from her first marriage. Her sister and her sister's husband moved to San Diego to be close to her.

The relationship between Sadie and Beezie had become lax because of the distance between Los Angeles and San Diego. We also started traveling. About four years after Ray left we got a call from her sister that Beezie had died.

Ray never worried too much about anything. The main reason he did well with me probably was because he enjoyed it. He was a very charismatic individual who could get away with anything. You forgave him. I don't think Beezie was even mad at him. He had a glow about him. He was likable. He was easy to be with. He always laughed. You don't run into people like that very much. He was a likable rogue. He didn't always do everything "according to Hoyle."

Chapter 20: Charlie Mesnick

We traveled extensively with some friends of ours, the Mesnicks. Charlie Mesnick's wife, Dora, Sadie and I went to high school together. Dora was blind in one eye. She attracted my attention at school because she talked back to the teacher and nobody does that. She didn't like the teacher in home room. I guess Dora had nothing to lose because there was no grading. It could be that the teacher didn't like Dora either. The first thing when we gathered in home room and everybody sat down, the teacher would say something to Dora. And then Dora would get up and talk back to her. She seemed nice otherwise. It took a lot of guts to do that; I would never do that. As time went on you found out she was just having fun as far as she was concerned. She was the only girl in a family of five children; she had four brothers and so she sort of ran the show because she was the only girl. She became aggressive; she thought she could do anything she wanted. Her father had a bakery.

She went to Cleveland and met Charlie. He was a graduate of Western Reserve College in Cleveland. He had a degree in Social Service Administration like my brother Manny. He was a good student. He graduated from high school at 16. I think there was a matchmaker involved. Dora's father was a pretty rich man. He ran the Detroit Jewish bakery on Brooklyn Ave. in Boyle Heights. We met Charlie one year after we were married, but before they were married. They were married about four years after us, in '37. We went to their wedding.

They got married at the Jewish Home for the Aged on Boyle Avenue and 4th Street which specialized in catering to weddings and bar mitzvahs. They had a hall there where you could have dancing and a band. It was big enough to have a nice, good sized party. They had to have good food. It was fancy. Our wedding was simple compared to this.

They lived in Los Angeles. During the war Charlie was in the Navy stationed at Salt Lake City. Dora was with him. So we lost contact during the war. Dora was friends with Sadie and considered me a friend because I was in her classroom. Dora and Sadie knew each other from childhood. They were the same age and went to kindergarten and grade school, and junior high together. I didn't meet Dora until eleventh grade because I wasn't here. We were all in the same grade.

We didn't see them during the war, but after the war there was a high school reunion and we became friendlier. Around '45 Dora bought a bakery on Pico Blvd and did very well. She knew the business and had a partner. The Bakery is still in business today. It's called the Beverlywood Bakery, two blocks west of Doheny on Pico in Los Angeles. Charlie ultimately became the head of the Los Angeles Jewish Centers. His office was at the Westside Jewish Center on Olympic. They had two sons, one of whom did very well in sales for Gallo Wine.

You had to be able to afford to travel, and they were able to travel with us.

When Charlie traveled he had a list of people to see, and so we saw them. Charlie was the director, or executive vice president of the Jewish Community Center Association. The president of

Join the
'Salute to
Charlie Mesnick'

Sunday, November 9, 1975
6:30 P.M.
Grand Ballroom
Beverly Hilton Hotel
Program prepared by   Shimon Wincelberg
Master of Ceremonies   Bert Gold
Music   Manny Harmon

R.S.V.P. Enclosed

the organization was elected and titular, the man who gave the most money to maintain the facility. Charlie opened up about six Jewish Community Centers in the Los Angeles area.

The heads of the Jewish Community Associations around the world communicated with each other. Every three or four or five years they would have a convention where they met some place. They would exchange information. A lot of people from around the world Charlie had met before, at these conventions. When the conventions were in Los Angeles he would be involved in entertaining these people. Because we were friends, we would be invited to Charlie's house when he was entertaining some of these people from around the world. In Palm Springs during the '80's we bought two units next door to each other at the Firebird Condominiums, where my brother Manny and his wife also bought one.

Charlie always managed to have lunch with his donors at the Jewish Country Club even though he was not a member. The membership was about $25,000. All the Jewish actors were members. Charlie had to maintain a certain façade for his work.

When a friend like Charlie has an important position in the world, it's sometimes surprising because you know him socially and better than anyone else. He was very respected in the world Jewish community. He kept in touch with the Jewish leaders of the world. There was no reason not to like him. We played a very important part in each others' lives. In front of me he did not have to play a part. That's why I knew him better than anybody else could. I was a tremendous relief for him. I was rewarded, in a manner of speaking, by the people I was able to meet.

In New Zealand, we met Dora's cousin who owned a famous nightclub restaurant called "The Troika" which in Russian means a team of three horses (to pull a sled or wagon). He took a lot of time out to show us New Zealand. He made special arrangements for us to see the New Zealand Kiwi bird which is only in New Zealand. Apparently they are a night bird because they woke them up for us to see them.

In Australia we met Charlie's counterpart, the head of the Australian Jewish Centers. We were invited to dinner at their house. Having me along helped Charlie make a good impression. I was a good companion at these parties; someone he knew he would not be ashamed of. I might have a discussion with a difference of opinion without it being an argument. I believe everybody is entitled to their own opinion. I never force my opinion on anyone else.

Traveling with Charlie, through his connections, we were involved with local situations which one wouldn't come across as just a visitor, or tourist. In Northern Africa Charlie had his list of people-to-see so when we went to Morocco we met the king's doctor. That was very interesting. The king of Morocco was not anti-Jewish. The people were, siding with the Muslims over the Israeli situation.

There were a lot of Jews celebrating Saturday, the Sabbath, in Morocco. Being Jewish, we were invited to Sabbath dinner in Tangiers at the home of the head of the Jewish Community there, who was Orthodox. Orthodox Jews celebrate Saturday. In fact, Saturday is the most holy day except Yom Kipper and Rosh Hashanah. It's one of the Ten Commandments: you work six days and you must rest on the seventh.

Charlie and our host talked about a lot of things to do with Jewish life. When we arrived at his house our host was wearing a tuxedo with a coat and tails, very formal. We were dressed in street clothes. We didn't carry formal clothing on this kind of overland trip, as we did on board ship. I think our host was under the impression, from watching old movies produced in the '30's, that Americans wore tuxedos all the time. All the movies had people in tuxedos. Prior to that, the silent movies they were showing "real people" in tuxedos. I would say in American movies, if it wasn't a cowboy movie, it was a tuxedo movie.

We probably had the traditional Jewish Sabbath meal called Cholent. My mother would make it sometimes but not with the grandeur of my mother-in-law. Cholent is an Orthodox Jewish meal. You cooked it on Friday so that you could eat it on Saturday. It was a very delicious meal, consisting of barley, chicken and roast. Everything got cooked, probably overcooked. It came in a soup tureen. You had it for lunch and you had it for dinner. And you had it for dinner the night before because it was ready Friday night and it took 24 hours to cook. We had some kind of chicken which probably came from a Cholent.

Chapter 21: Saber Air Freight

The third business I started was air freight. When you're in business people ask, "Can you do this? Can you do that?" If you can do it, you do it, if you can't do it, you don't do it. When I was doing freight distribution with Sav-On Freight one of my customers was American Greetings who made greeting cards. Their company was in Cleveland, Ohio and they shipped out of the Cincinnati Airport which is not in Ohio; it's in Kentucky. They wanted to ship their stuff by air because greeting cards have to be put on display long before the holiday. The biggest holiday for greeting cards was Valentine's Day. The second one was Mother's Day and the third one was Christmas. The cards have to be in the stores way beforehand and they wanted to air ship four or five containers at a time. They were having trouble with the commercial airlines so we applied and got a license to be an air freight forwarding company. I did this to accommodate this one customer. I called the company Saber Air Freight. This was in the late 60's.

Freight forwarding is a service that accepts freight from shippers and arranges for that freight to be shipped to the destination requested. Sav-On Freight was a distribution service. That's a service that accepts consolidated shipments from a shipper and breaks the consolidated shipment into the individual shipments and delivers them to the consignees. It's really the opposite of freight forwarding. Freight forwarding handles outbound freight and freight distribution handles inbound freight.

The name "Saber" came by combining our names, Sadie and Bernie. My general manager, Murphy suggested the name. I came up with the logo which was two sabers, interlocking them so that the handles of the two sabers created an "S".

I didn't stay in Air Freight long. I had Sav-On Freight and Universal Mail Delivery going. The reason I went into air freight was to accommodate one customer. I didn't know anything about it except superficially. I gave it to my son to learn the business. My son, Bob, had just graduated from Long Beach State with a degree in business administration and I said, "You learn about it." He learned about it and ran it for five years before I gave the business to him.

We hired a guy from an air freight company who was a salesman and knew something about it. Bob and he developed it. Bob needed a business and he wanted the air freight business. We had offices in different cities; Seattle, Portland, Salt Lake City, Phoenix, and L.A. We contracted to local trucking companies but managed from our home office. Bob met his present wife at Sav-On Freight. They worked in the same office.

While Bob was working for me before I gave him the business, he didn't show up for work one day. I said you can't do that and bawled him out. He became indignant and said "The heck with you." and quit. He went to work in the shoe business in Sherman Oaks for several months and met his first wife there. She was a customer. After a few months he came back. He had made the point that he could get a job on his own. But being a shoe clerk was not what he wanted for a career. He liked the transportation business.

He was working with an emphasis on Saber Air Freight. He had been learning the transportation business because he was working at Sav-On as well as Saber Air Freight and he helped out when he could in the Mail Delivery business.

He liked Saber Air Freight but he didn't like what the manager we hired was doing. The manager was charging high rates and taking the traffic managers to Vegas or to high class restaurants. In other words, they were both stealing from their companies. Let's say my normal rate would be $100. Maybe it would cost me 80 dollars for overhead. He knew that and so did the customers. What he would do is talk the buyer (not the owner) into more money and for that he would take the guy out maybe once a month somewhere he couldn't afford to go himself. After all, he was in control; he was showing Bob how to run the business. And he had his own kickback from Saber because he would charge for expenses in addition to his salary. Bob didn't like it. It was corrupt. It wasn't good for expansion because the guy was only dealing with corrupt traffic managers. The cost of this type of corruption is ultimately passed on to the last user of the commodity. It's not good for the economy. It's not fair and it's cheating.

Bob wanted the guy to go out and get more business but the guy said, "Hey, I'm doing well now. Why do I want to go out and sell?" His ambition was limited. This guy was taking advantage of Bob. There are some salesmen that are always able to bring along customers. He had brought these corrupt customers along with him. It didn't really matter to him. If we fired him, he would go to work with someone else and these three guys would follow him.

Once Bob realized what was going on, they got into an argument and Bob asked me to fire him. I told the guy that we would handle the bookkeeping and he could go out and get some more business. He quit, so I didn't have to fire him. He knew what was going on and he knew it wouldn't work out unless he ran the business. This was after about the first six months. Then Bob handled it on his own and learned much more as he went along. He hired other salesmen and watched to see that they didn't pull this sort of thing. Bob did very well.

The mail delivery service business didn't require much of a dock. The air freight did. The property in Inglewood had a warehouse on it and a little house. After Bob got married to Jeanne, who he met selling shoes, he lived in the little house for maybe six months. As time went on he got an apartment somewhere else. When Bob began to expand I had the house knocked down and in its place I built a metal facility and accommodated him with three trucking doors. He was doing very well. Later that became too small and I built him a 10,000 square foot warehouse with six loading doors for the distribution of air freight on the back part of the acre lot. We kept the annex for storage. When you're in the freight business you end up storing a lot of stuff. People refuse stuff then you have to put it in storage and notify the shipper that they refused it. Or they send it COD and the recipient won't pay for it. Sometimes you get a customer who wants you to distribute stuff a bit at a time. Stuff begins to accumulate. Sav-On freight had the same problem.

I didn't get too involved in Bob's business. I found that I was diluting myself into three businesses and I wasn't effective in any of them. I have maybe eight hours of productive time a day. I can use that time two hours here and two hours there but each one of the three businesses is getting two or three hours, not eight hours. If I concentrate my efforts on one business, I will be more effective and more productive. I ran Sav-On Freight and Murphy managed Universal Mail. Bob ran Saber Air Freight.

Chapter 22: The Travel Bug

I started the business in '53 and in '58 the business was off and running: five years into it and I was ready to travel. I had about 200 accounts, with 20 or 30 employees. I was soliciting for new accounts every day. We went on an ocean liner to Hawaii to celebrate our twenty-fifth wedding anniversary. We had a bon voyage party with champagne in our cabin. This was our first big party. We had been pretty well suppressed because we never had the funds. Then all of a sudden we did have them. We wanted to celebrate it and we wanted to share it.

We took off from Wilmington and were gone ten days. This was our first major trip. It took five days to sail there and we flew back on Pan Am. Sadie's brother, Jerry, had gone to Hawaii two months before. He gave us all kinds of information; restaurants to go to, places to see. We did everything he did. We stayed at the Waikiki Hawaiian Village. The last meal we had there was enjoyable. We were so sick and tired of gourmet meals that we went to a drugstore lunch counter and had a hamburger. That was the best tasting meal of the whole trip.

We were bitten by the travel bug. Travel became a part of our life. The next year (1959) we went to the Caribbean. From then on we traveled at least once a year and eventually as much as four times a year. We went to every country in Europe except Albania which you couldn't enter because of Communism. We went to every continent. We visited a lot of countries in Africa, mostly in East Africa. We visited every country except Bolivia in South America. We visited almost every country in Asia. We visited Japan about four times. We covered as much of the world as we could. We were very fortunate that we were able to do that and I have no regrets whatever.

My business was growing on a sharp, steady, upward incline. I had followed the old business adage, "Find a need and fill it." I had two employees who really ran the show once I got it going. They ran it and they ran it efficiently and profitably. I was able to go whenever I wanted. In '68 I sold the house on Goodland and, after living in a very nice apartment on Fulton in Sherman Oaks for a year, I bought a condominium in Beverly Hills that we could lock and leave. You can't really do that with a house.

We started traveling far and wide through the years, sometimes and more often in the later years of our marriage, cruising on ships. We went on more than a hundred cruises. Manny and I took our extended families together on two cruises to Mexico as family reunions.

Sav-On Freight was well on its way and so was Universal Mail Delivery Service. We had some very nice offices by then, including one in Coldwater Canyon. Through Saber Air Freight we belonged to an association where we got 75% off on airline tickets. We traveled first class all the time because 75% off on first class was almost as cheap as going coach. The association was called International Air Transport. Once you're in it, you're in it. The airlines gave good rates to members of the association because they wanted their air freight business.

Sadie could buy whatever she wanted after my business was established. She enjoyed dressing and had some nice outfits when we traveled. I never noticed much but from the photographs one can see her talent for flair. One outfit she liked was black and white polka dots. She liked hats. Women's hats reflect eras. You can tell the era by the style of the hat. If she liked what she was wearing, I liked it. I'm not a maven for women's styles so I don't have any opinion about women's hats or clothing.

Our marriage was kept interesting by our traveling. We made friends with whom we kept in touch over the years. We had a lot of Jewish friends because that was the area of our travel, at home and abroad with Charlie. However we made friends from outside that circle when we were out in the world traveling by ourselves, which we did more often than not. Not everybody could go when we wanted to go. They had their obligations. Sadie and I began to drift towards people who could afford to travel also. Sometimes that would create resentment.

Hong Kong

When you visit many places in Asia, like India, Thailand, or anywhere southward, say, Australia, or Indonesia, or Singapore, you go through Hong Kong. And we figured, since we're going through, we might as well stop over a few days.

In Hong Kong we spent time with a connection of our friend Charlie Mesnick. There was a young man who worked for Universal Studios who was the son-in-law of a studio magnate, Run Run Shaw, in Hong Kong, one of the world's leading movie producers, making about 180 films a year, mostly blood-and-guts 'Eastern' Westerns. And Charlie knew someone from Universal Studios who suggested the connection. The wife was in Hong Kong, so we called her when we were there. She was our hostess for most of the time and spent about three days with us, showed us where to shop, and introduced us to shopkeepers who paid more

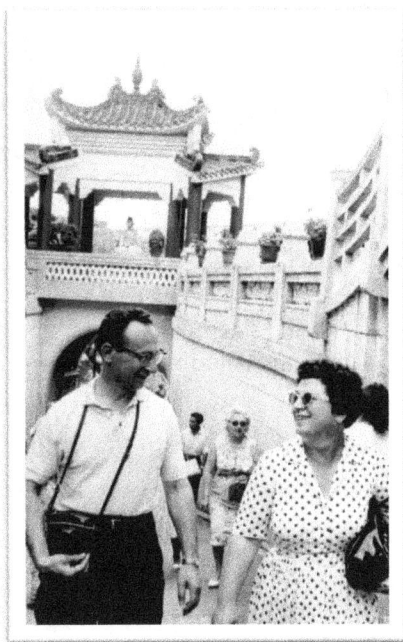

In China with Sadie

attention to us than they normally would have. (Their asking prices, however, went up because of our association with a very rich woman.) Our hostess took us to lunch, and made suggestions for interesting places we might want to go see. We traveled with Charlie Mesnick and his wife Dora most of the time.

When we were walking around Hong Kong there was a Rolls Royce that was following us very slowly. Dora, said, "I think we're being followed." The young woman, the wife of the young man at Universal Studios, said, "Oh, that's Joe. He's our chauffeur."

We would stay at the Peninsula Hotel whenever we could. The Peninsula is actually in Kowloon, and Kowloon is across the bay from Hong Kong. Kowloon was part of the British Colony, and because it was developed later, it was more modern. Hong Kong itself didn't have that many hotels. The Peninsula Hotel was close to the ferry which went to Hong Kong.

Service at the Peninsula was excellent and the furnishings were also very nice. It was well located and had a good restaurant. By Kowloon standards it was expensive, but by our standards it was affordable. I would say it's one of the best and most famous hotels in the world. In fact, it was the number one hotel in the world at the time. Whenever we booked at The Peninsula it would include an airport pick up, and they picked us up in a Rolls Royce.

We really liked Hong Kong and went there at least 20 times. I saw Hong Kong grow up! The first time we were there the women were paving the main street in Kowloon, Nathan Road. They were putting cobblestones into cement. By the time we were through with our visits they had repaved the street with cement. They also built an underground metro subway, a highway, and a major bridge. Within about 20 years they had made it so that you could take the subway to Hong Kong, take the ferry, or drive across. Government-wise, it didn't take forever to get something done. Once they decided to do something, they got it done. It was an exciting city in all respects. I never saw anything happen as quickly as it did there. For example, they say 'Let's build a subway!' Okay, it's done. Here they talk about building a subway for five years before they say yes or no. In Hong Kong they didn't have time to waste. In any case, Hong Kong was going to be handed over to the Chinese and it became a role model for

China. I saw something grow up before my eyes in 20 years that in L.A. might take 200 years. We still don't even really have a subway.

There was a village near Hong Kong called Stanley Village. Stanley Village had a marketplace that sold almost anything at reduced prices. In the beginning of our visits it was sort of a raggedy shopping area, sort of like our farmer's markets here. There were open air stalls. A few years later we went there and there were buildings with the same shops. The prices were still relatively good. The third time there they had a storefront with a glass door. Over time it was gradually upgraded and became a very modern, fancy shopping area (instead of having to walk around in the mud if it happened to rain). It was fun and interesting to go there for a number of reasons. They had floating restaurants tied to the docks on the Kowloon side where you picked out the fish you wanted from a tank. They would net it on the spot and cook it the way you wanted: fried, boiled or baked and it was very good.

There was a lot to do in Kowloon. There was plenty of entertainment and a museum of modern science. Sadie had a good jeweler she liked and I had a good tailor in Kowloon. There was great shopping and a lot of different restaurants. In Kowloon we took a bus to a farm area where they wore very wide rimmed black hats with decorations around the edge. Every time they moved, the decorations would move and keep the flies away. There were a lot of interesting things to see.

On Wednesdays in Kowloon they would have a jade sale. The vendors would have their wares on the sidewalk for a whole block. They had all kinds of sizes and colors. If you liked something, you picked it up, and if the price was right, you bought it. It was cheap, but bargaining was expected, so you bargained. The pieces weren't set. You would take the piece to a jeweler and have it set, which could cost you twice as much as the stone.

They have a recipe in Hong Kong where they take a great big chicken, de-feather it and clean it and so forth and so on and they put it in this mud. In the mud they put the chicken in the oven and the mud crisps; the water evaporates out of it and maybe after two hours the chicken is done. They put it on the table; you hit it and the mud falls away. Very succulent chicken. The mother of our hostess presided over the table in a private room. We sat around and the mother would serve us with her chopsticks, the same chopsticks she would eat with!

Russia

We liked visiting Kiev for the delicious Chicken Kiev. It's full of butter. It's not good for you, but it tastes good. Sadie liked Chicken Kiev so we ordered it pretty often.

On our first trip to Russia, we were on our own. We arrived in Moscow, and by the time we got to the immigration check, which was our last delay before exiting to the street, we looked down the hallway where there was a barrier. On the other side of the barrier were a lot of people awaiting the arrival of their friends and relatives. Right in the first row, leaning against the barrier, were my two aunts. One was Branchik, the twin to my Aunt Itka, who lived in Los Angeles, and the other was Aunt Anka, who looked very much like my mother. The funny thing was, how did they know who we were? They seemed to know us. In any case, when we were released from immigration, we went directly to them. We hugged each other as though we were long lost relatives, which we were. The thing is, we recognized each other. There was some magic about it.

We then got in a cab for a long drive to the hotel. On the way, the cabbie would speed up to about 80 miles an hour and then he would put the gear shift in neutral and coast until it got to about 20 miles an hour and then he would put it back in gear and speed up again. Apparently he thought it was a good way to save fuel.

When we got to the Metropole Hotel in Moscow right around the corner from the Bolshoi Theatre, before we were able to get out of the car, we heard the "Thizzzzzz" of a flattening rear tire. Obviously the point here is that we were lucky it didn't happen five minutes earlier when we were up to 80 miles an hour. We might have been in a terrible accident. We realized we must have had a guardian angel with us. I would imagine the tires were very thin. Of course he might have hit a nail. You would have to be dumb not to realize your own luck.

My Aunt Anka had advised us not to talk politics anywhere in the cab or the hotel because it was assumed they were bugged. We went into the hotel and we were assigned a room on the fourth floor. We noticed that although there were two elevators, one of them was occupied by an elderly woman sitting on a chair behind an open card table. She would not accept any riders and kept pointing to take the elevator next to her. We waited for that elevator to come down so we could go up to our rooms. When we got to the fourth floor there was another registration desk. One of the clerks went with us to our room and gave us our key. In our room we put some things away and sat and talked a while about our relatives and how everybody was. We decided to go out and have some dinner. So we went to the elevator and the first elevator that opened up was the woman who told us to take the next elevator. You pushed a button and the first available elevator would come up. You had a 50-50 chance of getting the lady. It was a good thing that she got to ride up and down because otherwise she would have been bored stiff sitting in such a confined space.

We had a very good dinner at the restaurant in the hotel. Any visitor to the USSR had to prepay for everything, especially tourists. In return, all hotels were prepaid and your food was prepaid by means of coupons, which were ample. You got plenty for your money. You paid for your breakfast, lunch and dinner with coupons. I probably paid out-of-pocket for my relatives. There were tourist rubles and regular citizen rubles. The tourist rubles had more value.

When we called for an elevator to return to our room, sure enough the card table lady came first. When we took the next elevator and went to the fourth floor to pick up our key from the fourth floor attendant, I asked her what the elevator lady's function was. She told me that this lady was a room service attendant. If you wanted room service, she would be the one who would get the meal and bring it to you. The four of us returned to our room and further discussed the next day's activities and things like that.

The following morning my two aunts showed up and so did my Uncle Archic. We had breakfast and my relatives began to show us around town. One day we went to the Moscow Circus and saw the Russian Dancing Bear and some great trapeze acts. I was sitting next to my Aunt Anka and when the trapeze artists were flying through the air, she would look away because she didn't want to see them fall. I do know that they thoroughly enjoyed the circus.

We went down to look at the beautiful underground metro station. There wasn't anything in Russia that was any more beautiful. It was well designed by an interior decorator - everything in there was very expensive. The government had paid a lot of attention to it. The trains were always on time. It looked like the living room of a castle. It was a source of pride for the people, the Muscovites.

The USSR was a communist country with a lack of freedom in many areas, but at least you had the freedom of being who you were without animosity. The anti-Semitism of early years did not seem as prevalent as it had been. For that reason, it was easier to tolerate the situation and furthermore, you knew you didn't have to tolerate it very long because you were going home.

I took Sadie to the Bolshoi (Bolshoi means 'big') which is an opera house where we saw Pagliacci. We also saw the Bolshoi Ballet. At the break at the opera they served vodka and rye bread with caviar. Usually when you have caviar it's on a little square. This time it was on half a slice of rye bread and you went around taking bites until it was gone.

That evening I decided to test the bugging operation in the hotel. I said to Sadie in a loud tone that we'd had a very nice day—Moscow was a beautiful city—the subways were great. I finally went on to the subject of the lady in the elevator and expressed my curiosity as to why she doesn't accept passengers. I said it would increase the service factor of the hotel. That was about it.

The next morning when we went down to the lobby to meet our relatives again, pushed the button, and low and behold, there was the lady in the elevator. We stood there expecting her to point to the next elevator. Instead, she motioned for us to come in. She took us down to the lobby. We met our relatives and I told them what happened and said, "It's true. There's no doubt, we're being bugged."

When we left we had enough coupons to buy a five-pound can of caviar to take home. My mother had done the same thing on her trip to Moscow and had advised me.

Buenos Aires

Sadie and I went to visit my mother's first cousin, Jake Schwartzstein (a son of the twelve Schwartzsteins), in Buenos Aires, Argentina. After his arrival in New York he went to New Jersey and then Los Angeles. We knew him very well.

He had a "customer service." He had connections with different wholesalers. Whatever you needed, he could get what you needed wholesale. To poor people, this was

Bermuda 1987

convenient shopping because he gave them credit. He created relationships.

For example, radios started. He bought them radios. Except that if they wanted to buy a radio and the radio cost 20 dollars, he might say, "give me ten dollars down and pay me a dollar a month." To protect himself, the down payment was the wholesale price. So he always got his money back. That way it was easy for him to extend credit. Most things have a hundred per cent mark up. He enabled you to buy what was needed at a reasonable price and pay it off on credit. He got the ten dollars. He didn't have to worry about anything.

In his case, he had no overhead. He didn't have a store or rent to pay or all the other stuff to pay, and people called him at home if they needed something. If you paid it off, he would say, "Do you need anything else, maybe some towels?"

I would imagine he had two or three hundred customers. He went door to door. He worked Mexican neighborhoods or the poorer neighborhoods; people who could pay a dollar a week without that much problem. He wouldn't lose anything if they disappeared. He was in that business for many years.

From Los Angeles he retired to a Jewish community in Buenos Aires to be with his four siblings who had emigrated there and not to the United States. My mother never met them. When he retired at 65 and became eligible for Social Security he felt that living in Buenos Aires would give him a better life for his money, and it did.

He had a nice apartment. However, he was disappointed that his brothers and sister didn't give him the attention that he thought they would. He was depending on his siblings. But he could only depend on them so much. His wife had died and his children didn't go with him to Argentina. He had a housekeeper and was single at that time. He was fine. He thought that now that he was free he would join his siblings and they would have fun. Well, he wasn't part of their "circle." He was an "extra man," a threat perhaps. They treated him like a "guest." After a while they went their own way. He was retired and his siblings were still working. He was all by himself. He did whatever he had to do. I never heard from him or saw him since then. He seemed to enjoy it. His money went further. We went to his apartment for a few hours and then we went back to our (touring) group. We deliberately took that particular trip so that we could visit him. He was very glad to see us.

I commented to Jake that he must know a lot of Spanish. He responded, "not a word." He lived in a Jewish neighborhood because it was easier. However, he soon asked us how we liked his "apartemiento!"

North Africa

In Tangiers our guide, an Arab, knew a lot of things and he was with Charlie, Dora, Sadie, and me for a whole week. He took us to a room, an office on a second floor in which was filled with Torahs, strewn all over the place. They were storing Torahs they had pilfered from synagogues. The Muslins make a big deal about disrespect to the Koran but here was a room just strewn with Torahs. They care a lot about their religion and are very strict but they don't give a damn about anybody else's religion. The guide figured that we would be interested. I'm not sure he agreed with his co-religionists. Actually, being in North Africa, with a lot of Arabs, we found that they are a very loving people with each other.

Our guide knew where all the stuff was and he took us there. He took us to places that no tourist would normally see. In Marrakesh, Morocco, he took us to the Djemaa El Fnaa, the inner city square with an open market. Outside the market there were parking places for horses and donkeys. You paid the guy and he tied them to the stake.

When friends saw each other at the market, the men kissed each other in greeting. They come from all around. You wouldn't think they had a mean bone in their body. You wouldn't normally see things like that. We were in Morocco two or three times. One time with Charlie and his wife we met a rabbi, but he wasn't very nice. The first thing he did was ask Charlie for a loan. I liked Morocco. It was interesting.

The Djemaa El Fnaa market was several thousand years old and was also a place of entertainment. They had acrobats, singers, dancers, magicians, and drummers. Grandfathers, sons, daughters;

they were all in the same business of entertainment. They made their money from donations from the viewers. Most of the people are poor and illiterate.

Restaurants hire the dancers for entertainment in the evening. The main course is called couscous. They don't serve silverware. You eat with your hands. I liked Moroccan food. They knew how to cook chicken.

Most of the people were illiterate so storytellers were popular. The storyteller would put a rug on the ground and people, mostly children but there were grown-ups too, would sit down and listen to this fellow tell a story. We would sit down and while he told the story in Arabic, we watched the faces of the audience. They would light up or be sad or be glad. It was interesting to see the reaction. He would pass a plate along and everybody contributed. That's the way they made their living. He serialized the stories so people would come back. He would tell a story and then say, well, more tomorrow. Tourists would sit around on the rug also. Of course they didn't understand him, but they would put pennies in the plate.

Chapter 23: On Faith, Tradition, and Religion

My parents were Jewish but we were more concerned with tradition than religion. My parents liked to celebrate the Jewish holidays such as Yom Kippur, Rosh Hashanah and Passover, not as religious but as traditional celebrations; as affirmation of their cultural identity. My father requested that when he died he not have a religious ceremony. When he died in 1962 we had a memorial service where people got up and spoke about him, saying nice things. We had it in the small auditorium of the "Workman's Circle" place. All of his friends gathered there.

My father knew the Bible, the Old Testament, by heart, which he learned at the chaider and he could recite from memory. He was a free thinker. He studied the Talmud, which teaches analysis of the Bible. He was skeptical about religious faith, being of a pragmatic nature. My mother and father believed in social equality and I would term their philosophy "Socialistic." My grandfather Reznick was religious because he sent my father to Hebrew school every day and my father learned the whole Bible in Hebrew, as well as mathematics and other things.

Maybe that's why my father wasn't religious. He read the Bible and figured, "Well, this is a nice story but I doubt that it happened." It's not a matter of losing faith; it's a matter of analysis and coming to a conclusion, over a period of time. You say "This isn't right. God doesn't kill people; but people are getting killed all the time. Here I am a Jew; I'm a religious Jew; I believe in God. What's the matter with God? He's not protecting me! He's letting the muzhiks have a field day killing Jews! What kind of a God is that?" I think he came to the conclusion that it was just a lot of baloney! Being born into the Jewish ethnicity, you don't necessarily agree to follow that religion. I'm not religious in any sense of the word except that I believe there's some power out there.

You accept the situation of life as futile and temporary. By realizing that you act accordingly, living your life the best you can, finding the means to do that. You're not going to live forever so you might as well make the best of it. I want the world to be happy and it's not. That makes you feel a little bit desperate on one hand and surrendering on the other. You're surrendering desperately to what the facts really are. My view is that if it can't be proved (scientifically), an idea has to be taken on faith. I don't have faith. My parents didn't have "faith." I wasn't brought up to have faith — I have just observed what goes on in the world. On the other hand, to get across the frozen river, my parents had to have faith in themselves.

The communities my parents lived in were generally Jewish neighborhoods and the woman I married, Sadie Marton, was Jewish. (Her name was adapted from the Hungarian "Serena." They had a choice of Sarah or Sadie and they wound up with Sadie.) Because she was traditionally Jewish, Sadie insisted on going to Temple on Yom Kippur and Rosh Hashanah. Did Sadie have faith? I don't know. She wanted to go to Temple because it was the thing to do. She was not kosher, so she was not religious. But did she have faith? Maybe; I don't know. The thing is, that both of us being "Jewish," that's all that really mattered.

Sadie's father must have had a lot of faith. When things were at their worst during the Depression he moved from Boyle Heights to Wilshire and La Brea area and organized a Temple. Ultimately, there was a movie house on West Pico called the Stanley Theater that they rented for his congregation on Rosh Hashanah and Yom Kippur. They never had enough people to worry about a regular meeting place. As a result Sadie had a certain amount of religion embedded. On religious holidays we went to services. I would go reluctantly because I thought the whole thing was a bunch of nonsense. The rabbi gives a sermon and they do a lot of praying out of the book, which I don't understand. As far as I was concerned most of the time I was bored stiff. I put up with it because that's what Sadie wanted. She wanted to go for the general principle. She felt that she should go whether she could read the book or not. She was "religious" but she didn't stick to the rules because they were nonsense.

For example, Sadie did not keep a kosher house. I don't even think her mother kept a kosher house. That's one of the rules of the Jewish religion. For example, you don't eat bacon and you follow the rules, if that's your religion. A long time ago they also decided you couldn't mix meat and dairy, because it didn't digest properly. Well, obviously it's not true, because people have been mixing cheese and all kinds of dairy with meat and it doesn't matter. But that's one of the rules. That's part of keeping kosher, like Catholics eating fish on Fridays. The biggest irony of all is that you can't have meat and dairy dishes touching each other. You can't eat them at the same time. If you touch meat with milk, you can't eat it. Milk comes from a cow...a cow is meat! It doesn't make sense.

After the war we joined the Temple over on Olympic because all of our friends belonged there. We had a social life through Sadie's involvement with the "Sisterhood" organization at the Synagogue. They had husbands and the men became friends. The Sisterhood would have lunches on Sundays and they would have a "sing-along." Most of us didn't know the words so they had song sheets and everybody sang together. This was around 1947-48, when we lived at my folks' apartment on 6th and La Brea.

Years later, Charlie Mesnick and I also went to a Bible class through the synagogue on Crescent Drive and Fountain that was interesting as a history class reading the Bible. It was run by a professor at the University of Judaism. He was a rabbi. It was an interesting class, about two hours. Sometimes we read one sentence and spent the whole two hours discussing it. The idea was that it was a history class and the Bible was a history book. These people actually lived there and this is what happened and some of it was exaggerated. No religion came out of it. The rabbi didn't do very much talking because whatever he said instigated a lot of speculation from all of the students.

We read the whole Bible. It took five years. Then they started all over again. Gradually I stopped going because I was too busy at work. The more I learned about the universe and the world, the less religious I became. What I mean by not being religious is that I stopped going to the Synagogue. It doesn't mean that I don't believe there's something out there that controls the Universe.

I still have contact with people from the Temple, though not very many, because my contemporaries have died. They keep in touch; I still know the rabbi there. He officiated at Sadie's funeral. I'm a member. They send me requests for money all the time.

As a matter of fact, my friend Mae and I have a mutual friend, Ruth Davis, who has been a member as long as we have; since it started there. At the Temple, they were honoring her with a lunch. Different people got up and talked. I went, but that's the first time I've been there in maybe two or three years.

It's a community affair, really. I find that a lot of people that are church people really associate with the church for social reasons more so than for religious reasons. A friend of ours, Beezie, came here from Wyoming. She's a Methodist. So she found a Methodist Church and joined it. She was never really religious, from anywhere I could see. But it was a good social place. When you come to a brand new town and you don't know anybody, you go to church. If you were an atheist, you wouldn't look for it.

I'm not an atheist. I just have a different idea of what religion is. I feel that most religions are man-made. Some of them have no basis for existing the way they do. I do feel that there's something out there a lot bigger than we are. Believe me, if there is somebody out there, I don't want to bother Him. The only other alternative out there is Mother Earth. Mother Earth and God might very well be the same function. I try to be good to people and I try to observe the rules and regulations of social living, of communal living. Whatever it is, you have to take care of each other.

Because of the freedom of association that exists in this country, everyone has an opportunity to meet anybody. Most parents prefer that their children marry within their own religious sect. That's one problem that wouldn't exist in the marriage. The problem that the Jews have is that they represent less than 3% of the population of the United States, which means that statistically, out of every hundred girls, only 3 of them are Jews. By the same token, for every hundred boys, only 3 are Jews. The odds are against their marrying their own kind.

There is a political reason for religion. People have to be controlled, otherwise there is chaos. By making people responsible to a god who is going to punish you if you're not good, there is control. You give a lot of thought to religion at my age. You try to analyze it. If there is a god, he has his own agenda.

It is been hard for me to understand why Jews are disliked. That's the whole objective of religion and that's why I think religion is a stupid exercise, because it creates animosity. Christianity is supposed to be about "Love thy neighbor" but they don't. They ignore the Christianity of the Christian religion. Next thing you know you have enemies instead of friends and you're supposed to develop friends. It doesn't make sense.

From the Jewish point of view, Christianity doesn't make sense. Once they began to listen to it, the first thing they come across is "Ignore the first commandment." The first commandment says "I am thy God, thy only God. Thou shall not have other Gods before me. They should not have idols before me." What happens, all of a sudden, God is in third place. Mary's in first place and they have Jesus in the second place and God's in third. He's the third guy. There wasn't supposed to be anybody, except one God. The Christians messed up the first commandment.

I have always wondered why the symbol for Christianity is a cross. The cross is a symbol of the worst kind of punishment there is, the worst kind of execution. They could have used the triangle, representing the trinity. Let's assume a religion is good, or is a believable fact; then you should have a logo that means something, like a circle that means eternity. Why honor the cross that killed Jesus? If he had been executed in an electric chair, would the electric chair be the symbol for Christianity?

Different people have different attitudes. In the Christian religion you know you go to heaven. Okay, you don't see it happen but you assume it's true and that it's happening. You accept the situation the way it is. It's not a tragedy. It's sort of a transition.

In the Jewish tradition, they say, "Well, when the Messiah comes, then you will be awakened." I don't know how they figure that, because the body disintegrates into nothing. So it's kind of a mysterious situation.

Some people's idea, like Manny and Barbara's and formerly mine, is that "when you die, you die. That's the end of it." There's no longer any substance. You can see the body disintegrating and it becomes the bones. My attitude now is that though the life in that body is gone, the life is still alive. The body is a vehicle. Now it's going to go into another vehicle, another baby. I believe in reincarnation. People are born with certain abilities depending on where they come from; not just your parents. You inherit a lot of instincts from previous lives. I believe that each life experience contributes to your instincts, so that each time you're reborn, you're smarter; you have more equipment to face life's challenges.

I compare life to an automobile. When you drive the automobile, you are the spark of life. With you behind the wheel, the automobile becomes alive. It goes wherever you want it to go. The vehicle gets old and broken down. You dispose of it and get another car. When your body is used up, when you're old and decrepit, worn out, the spark leaves you and finds another vehicle. We think we're more important than we are. I think God is like a committee. I don't know whether or not you have a choice of a body. Maybe you are scheduled. It's that type of program. It's not just helter-skelter. There has to be some sort of master plan. It doesn't have to be a God who is an individual.

If it's all one God, and you want to be religious, you say, well something's wrong with God. He's got three different major outfits out there and they all hate each other. Today, what's going on with the Arabs and the Christians and the Jews? Everybody hates each other. Is that something you want to believe in?

Bar Mitzvahs

I started studying for my bar mitzvah when I was 12, so that at 13, after six months to a year of going to Hebrew school once a week, I would be ready for my bar mitzvah ceremony. At the party I would read the chapter of the Bible in Hebrew pertaining to the week of my birthday. The Old Testament of the Bible consists of 52 different chapters, and when you go to Synagogue, they read the chapter for that particular week in Hebrew. At the end of the year, on the 52nd week, they read the last chapter and the next week on Rosh Hashanah, they start with chapter 1 again. Rosh Hashanah marks the beginning of the year.

When you read the Bible, you sing it, the idea being that when you talk to God, you don't talk to Him, you sing to Him. In other words, you have to change the kind of voice you use - you have to be "beautiful." So you learn the Hebrew passage for your bar mitzvah and the music that it requires. It's not a short piece – it may be a couple of pages that you memorize. The rabbi tells you how to sing it and you have to do it that way. Now don't forget, you don't study day after day. Maybe you go every Tuesday. By the time you come back a week later, you've forgotten most of what you learned because you weren't interested to begin with. Little by little you realize that just by rote you begin to understand it although it's not a short piece. When you finally read it at the party, even though you're reading it from a book, you know it because you've learned it by heart. Sometimes because you're excited - you're on stage, you forget. So that's why the book is there.

Hebrew school was competitive. You got a prize if you learned your passage well, and I have a competitive nature. I have always been proud of the medals I earned. Not that it's important to 'win', but it's important to get the job done. I won a five dollar gold piece. (I don't know what it would be worth today - I don't have it anyway.) That was my nature. I didn't care if I was learning English or Hebrew. The thing is I felt I should learn whatever it is that I'm doing.

When you have a bar mitzvah at 13 you're still a little kid. The indication is, from now on, you have to think like a man. You have to do it; you can't depend on your parents to do everything for you. You have to be independent and start to learn how to take care of yourself - you have to start to learn how to take care of a family, so that when you get married, you will have that experience. It's part of the general discussion. You're through with being a child and you start being an adult.

My son Marvin did not want to go through the rigmarole of a bar mitzvah and was openly defiant in his opposition to studying at the synagogue. I sent him to Hebrew school, but he played "hooky." When he was supposed to go to class he openly walked around in a building under construction in front of our house where we could see him. He didn't understand what it was all about and he didn't want to be bothered. However, we gave my son Bob an elaborate bar mitzvah party. Bob has always been interested in studying. After the bar mitzvah, Bob went about his business. He wasn't religiously Jewish; he was traditionally Jewish.

Chapter 24: Life and Business, Life and Death

I remember when I was about 11 in New Brunswick, milk was available only through home delivery because of refrigeration issues. The milk bottles had cardboard caps. On the cap was the company identification. At that time, kids were beginning to save milk bottle caps. I had some. One day there was something going down in the empty lot with a bunch of kids. I went down to see what was going on.

The kids were trading milk bottle caps. The milk bottle caps acquired different values depending on how many were around. So, we started trading. Based on demand and supply, the caps had different values. I got the best business experience because we were required to determine how many common caps you were willing to give away for some uncommon cap. At the end of the trading session, I had done very well. I went down with about fifteen caps and came back with a whole shoe box full. I would buy rare caps for some amount and turn around and sell higher, so I made a profit. The next day I woke up full of high expectation but the market for bottle caps crashed because not enough kids showed up to trade. Some kids lost all their caps. It was business, not gambling. You had to have business savvy. Anyway, interest fizzled. Maybe the mothers threw the caps away!

This experience had some influence in my attitude towards business. I wasn't afraid of it. Some people are afraid of going into business because they might lose their investment. What if you open up a store and there are no customers? If you have a negative attitude toward business risk, you're not going to gamble. Some people are good managers but don't want to risk their own money by managing their own business. For example, my manager Murphy was a good manager of my money and was comfortable getting a good salary. There's a saying in California, "You can't win the lottery without buying a ticket." That's what business is about.

In running any business, you have to pay attention to all of the aspects; advertising, sales, commissions, natural overhead, competition, accounting, etc. You should not favor one aspect over another. You have to control it all. You can't let your profit accumulate as money owed you. You reach a point where you owe money. Accounts receivable has to be paid attention to. You can't assume that everyone is going to pay their bills. There's always some guy that doesn't. You have to stop doing business with them.

I was motivated to succeed in business because I wanted to live better and I couldn't depend on anybody else. I had the poverty factor. It was the middle of the Depression. None of my kids had the poverty syndrome. You swim upstream all the time because you don't want to be in poverty. Like selling newspapers; I didn't really want to do all that but I did it to survive.

Motivation depends on an individual's circumstances, including personality makeup. Number one is to make a living; get a job. Number two is to do better than that by going into a small business. Each category has a different goal. You have the motivation of reaching a point where you're comfortable. You have the motivation to be more than comfortable and you have the motivation of becoming a billionaire purely because you want to reach that point, not because you can benefit any more than you can by being a millionaire. My father didn't want to have a big business. His motivation was satisfied when he was comfortable. My motivation was satisfied when I reached the point in business where I had a nice income and could do whatever I wanted. It's a personal level of comfort.

There are many people in our society who are satisfied just to get a job. They don't want responsibility. Their main goal is to drink beer and watch football. There's the segment of the population who are homeless. The problem with most of these people is that they don't save for the future. In some cultures people are taught to save half of their income for the future. This helps to avoid the homeless situation.

Unfortunately, a lot of people live above their income entirely. They feel secure and start buying boats, cars, trailers, etc., so that the payments take up every cent they make. They are unable to save a nickel. If they lose their job and go broke, they might not have a relative to move in with and so wind up homeless. Then it becomes harder than ever to get a job. You don't have an address. You have no stability. Employers are very careful about whom they hire.

Good management is a talent. What it doesn't need is two heads. I found out that with Sadie. I got a warehouse in North Hollywood for Sav-On Freight and she came to help me. I was the boss and she was the boss. I would give someone an order and she would counteract it for her own reasons without checking with me. For example, she would make a suggestion about changing something, and I had already taken care of it. At this time the business was just beginning to grow. From her point of view, she had the right to be a boss because she was part owner. After two or three days, I had to tell Sadie not to help me anymore. It had to be taken care of right away. Too many cooks spoil the broth.

The experience I had was rudimentary. It was pretty obvious. I realized that I had to make a living, very quickly. I had to pay rent. I had to feed and clothe my family. I had full responsibility for a wife and child at twenty years old. It was tough getting off the ground. I had factors in my favor. I was in good health. You have to live within your means; that's making a living. I was able to live within my means while I was building my business because I had retirement saved at the Post Office when I went out on my own. It takes an effort with initiative to get anywhere.

If you want something, you have to work for it. Even then there's no guarantee. If one way doesn't work, use an alternative way. My mother, for example, was resolute. There's a strong will to survive and you have to find a way to do it.

My business turned out to be a very positive thing as far as I'm concerned. It gave me the opportunity to put enough money away to retire without worrying. It gave me the opportunity to visit the whole world many times, many different places. There are still a lot of places I haven't been to but I've been to most. Sadie and I had a very good life together and we enjoyed the world as much as anybody could. If I had a hundred million dollars, I wouldn't have enjoyed it any more. A lot of money doesn't make the difference. What you need is not a lot of money but enough money.

I'm not afraid of dying now because, since Sadie died, I don't have anybody to protect anymore. I had to be around in order to take care of her. But once I lost control of her, once she was gone, what's to be afraid of? As of right now, when it comes, it comes. I'm not going to be worrying about it. I may be around another five years; I may be gone in six months, who knows? Since I'm part of eternity, it doesn't make any difference.

To me, at this point, death is freedom from the responsibility of living. At this point, I'm tired. I can't hear well; I can't see. My body is wearing out, so it's probably time. I'm not afraid of death. It doesn't seem as bad as it does when you're forty. You begin to ask "Why?" You begin to realize that religion is a self-induced hope. There's no truth to it. There's no nothing to it. It gives you an opportunity to stay alive with something, even though it's nothing. Death remains a mystery.

www.ingramcontent.com/pod-product-compliance
Lightning Source LLC
Chambersburg PA
CBHW020515100426

42813CB00030B/3250/J